O Lucky Man!

O Lucky Man!

Lindsay Anderson & David Sherwin

Plexus, London

All rights reserved including the right
of reproduction in whole or in part in any form
This edition copyright © 1973 by
Plexus Publishing Limited
Original screenplay entitled *O Lucky Man!*
copyright © 1973 by SAM
Published by Plexus Publishing Limited
18 Pentney Road,
London SW12
First printing 1973

ISBN 0 85965 001 4

Cover design by: John Marsh/Terence Porter

Manufactured in Great Britain by Highbury Press Limited

Contents

7   Preface
    Lindsay Anderson

10 Diary of a Script
    David Sherwin

23 Credits

26 The Script

Preface
Lindsay Anderson

A film script, it always seems to me, is a difficult thing to read. Unless you happen to have written it yourself. When David Sherwin and I had finished the original draft of *O Lucky Man!* we both thought it read pretty well. But I think this was chiefly because we were reading it, so to speak, from the inside. When I read the same document through today, I marvel that we were ever given the money to make it.

The script as presented here differs in many respects from that original draft. This version describes the completed film; and we have tried to make it vivid. A fair amount of material was cut before or during shooting, and these scenes, lines, episodes do not appear. Some of these losses were sad, some were not. The original conception, with extended scenes in the Coffee Factory and in Sutherland House, took too long to get "off the ground". Mick spent longer escaping from the Millar Clinic, and actually witnessed the fate of Elizabeth Valerie Stewart: this was appealing, but took up too much time. And near the end, after he has been set on and his benevolence finally smashed by the down-and-outs, we saw Mick wandering further, past mysterious midnight explosions, police whistles and the sound of running feet, before he met his destiny in Leicester Square. The evocation of contemporary urban malaise could have been powerful. But poetically the film certainly gained from concentration.

The early part of the tale, it's springboard so to speak, was largely the contribution of Malcolm McDowell, from memories of his early coffee-selling days in the North East. Alan Price's songs were all (except one) written and recorded before we started shooting;

although the original script had only indications of where each song should come, and what should be its general theme. The radio pieces are all "genuine", plucked out of the haunted air by the simple expedient of placing the microphone of my cassette tape-recorder in front of my transistor radio, usually early in the morning. The talk on Zen Buddhism was provided in this way, by the magic intervention of chance, only a few days before we were due to dub the reel.

One characteristic feature of *O Lucky Man!* is not conveyed by the script: I mean the continual reappearance of actors in different roles. This idea came with the writing of the script—so that Professor Stewart, for instance, was hardly imagined before he had the face, figure and peculiar vibrancy of Graham Crowden, and of course it would have to be Rachel Roberts, harking back to earlier triumphs, as the aggressive, defeated housewife who decides that she's had enough. We never indicated these repetitions in any version of the script, partly, perhaps, because we never wished to feel enclosed in a formula; and partly, in a strange way, because we felt that this wasn't anybody's business but ours. The choices were intuitive (like the monochrome sequences in *If. . . .*), never theoretical or 'programmed'. Chance also entered into it again because we could not afford to contract our entire company for the entire period of shooting: but it seemed quite appropriate that some of these reappearances should be (partly) fortuitous. And when Alan Price came up with his words for the last song, it all fell into place:

> On and on and on and on we go,
> Round the world in circles turning
> Earning what we can...

As anyone who knows *If. . . .* will surely recognise, this film is an organic development from that work of five years ago. Many, if not most, of the same creative talents were involved; and Malcolm McDowell is again playing Mick Travis ("was your headmaster correct to expel you from school?"). But development does not imply repetition; and if this Mick starts as considerably more naif (and more conventionally ambitious) than the character in *If. . . .* he ends up considerably wiser. Wisdom is still "the principal thing". Of course people must make their own judgements of the experience, and their own interpretations. Personally I can only say that he seems to me to arrive, after his journeying through the world of illusion, at some kind of acceptance of reality. But acceptance is not conformism.

April 3rd, 1973.

Diary of a Script
David Sherwin

6th March, 1969

Malcolm and I arrive in New York for the opening of *If*.... next Sunday. The air fares alone cost £298 each, but we haven't a cent in our pockets. A man from Paramount publicity meets us but he can't find our driver. The driver is asked on the public address system to present himself at the BOAC desk. After two appeals he appears. His feet slop forward over the marble as if he was trudging through mud in heavy army boots. He is pissed.

In the hotel Malcolm picks up the phone to order champagne and a pot of tea. A giant spark shoots out from the phone mouthpiece to his chin. The 'Captain'—the porter—tells us it is the wall-to-wall nylon carpeting—static electricity. Whenever we touch the door handles, or tv, or phone, sparks shoot out. The 'Captain' advises us to lift one foot off the ground before touching anything. Malcolm pours the tea, hopping on one foot. We have no money, so we order everything on room service. It costs three times as much, viz whisky $15 instead of 5 in the shops.

Over champagne and tea I tell Malcolm my idea for a story called *Manpower*—the story of a young man, perhaps an out-of-work ballet dancer. He works as a char doing different jobs on different days in different peoples' homes. He practices leaps while dusting.

Malcolm has also been working on a story about a character starting life at the bottom of the pile; something autobiographical and in some ways, he says, similar to mine . . . but before he can tell me we are interrupted.

The door bell rings. A wierdly dressed 'family' enter. There are three sons who seem about 30, very pale faces, black plastic macs or jackets and black rubber boots. They hold cheap plastic shopping bags containing instamatic cameras. They take Malcolm's photo and ask for his autograph. With them is a tall old lady in a macintosh whom they address as 'Mother'. One of the sons tells Malcolm, "She's English. She's a dame, she's a real dame from England. But with a small 'd' 'cos she's no lady. A dame, see?" They leave. Who are they? Journalists? Queers? How did they know we were in the hotel? We'd only arrived an hour ago.

Malcolm pours out another round of champagne and tells me his story, an idea he has been working on since he finished *If*. . . . It's called *Coffee Man* and starts in a coffee-making factory in Liverpool. The story follows the ambitions of a trainee salesman. There is no proper training and he has nothing to do all day. He wanders aimlessly around the factory floor with a clipboard for notes, chatting to the roasters, blenders, and coffee packing girls. Then one day he is suddenly sent off to Yorkshire in a battered van to replace a salesman who has vanished without notice. The hero ends up in London giving his life savings to a music teacher, a con man who promises to make him into a pop star. *Coffee Man* seems much more real than *Manpower*. Also Paramount, to whom the *Manpower* idea has been put are only prepared to pay £1,000 for the first draft, and it will be a couple of years work. Malcolm asks me to work on *Coffee Man* . . . I drop *Manpower*.

A year passes...

19th January, 1970
I type out the first 20 pages of *Coffee Man* up to the end of factory section—coffee sampling. Talk on the phone with Malcolm as to whether scene when Mick goes into packing room should include the line, "Christ, the girls in that room—they reek". Include it.

Show the 20 pages to Lindsay. He thinks it is too mini and naturalistic.
"Keep working on it," he says, "get it away from just being about selling coffee.—Have you read *Heaven's My Destination*? It's about a Bible salesman. Quite epic. Tails off at the end though. Why is it that writers can never write real endings? It's very odd—why is it?"

Friday, 21st August, 1970
At Malcolm's flat in the morning. Sunny outside. We talk to and fro, trying to find the essence of *Coffee Man*, trying to make it

'epic' for Lindsay...

Malcolm says—"I always remember Gloria Rowe, the Sales Director, who I used to talk to when I was training on the shop floor—I wasn't training—I was just walking around with a clipboard looking for something to do—she used to say to me 'Malcolm, you'll either be a Duke or a dustman.' And I'd always been told I was born with a silver spoon in my mouth. I always believed I would be lucky."

I jump up—

"That's it!"

"What?"

"Luck—luck's the essence. You've always believed you'll be lucky."

"Yes—luck—*Lucky Man*."

Sunday, 23rd August, 1970

Malcolm rings to say that he has arranged a meeting for two o'clock to see Lindsay to discuss *Lucky Man*. But he can't go. He has to go to rehearse his film with S. Kubrick. I must go alone.

I groan—"It'll be a disaster without you. You can recount the good episodes. You're the actor. You've got to be there... well then, let's put it off till you can go and we can all three meet."

"No, I've just rung him. He's in a very good mood. He's expecting you. You can talk to him better than I can."

Malcolm's psychological warfare. He has realised that two against one would make Lindsay antagonistic.

So I drink some whisky and write out a plot—the first thing Lindsay will say is—"What have you written? Why haven't you written anything? You're supposed to be a writer aren't you? What do you do all day?"

Lindsay opens the door. Gives a groan, a wry smile.

L: Malcolm's just been. He's quite batty. Left me a script to read. (The script of another project.) God I hate reading. Do I really have to?

D: Well it's very easy. It's better than the book.

L: I thought it looked bad—what have you written?

I screw up the plot in my pocket.

D: Nothing.

L: What? What's there to talk about if you haven't written anything? What have you been doing with Malcolm all this time?

D: Well we've been discussing it.

L: Discussing it!

D : Well, we've discovered the essence, what it really should be about, and also a style which makes it more than just a story about a salesman in coffee. Coffee would just be part of it. He'd do other things.
L : What other things? What essence.
D : Well it should be like *Heaven's My Destination* or *Amerika*. A series of things. And his character—like Candide. He believes he's lucky. Some of the time he is successful and then suddenly it all vanishes. But he thinks it doesn't matter. He's always been lucky. Something will turn up. And there's a girl—first she works for a den of thieves, the next adventure she's a chimney sweep—and . . .
L : You see, I think a series of adventures, this girl popping up—other characters popping up—it runs the risk of running away into the sands of—how can I say it?—into little sandhills—of something small scale. What is the character really after? What can anyone be after in a world where nothing spiritual matters anymore? What's he after?
D : I don't know. He just believes he's lucky. He's not like the hero of *Heaven's My Destination*. He hasn't got a mission.
L : Have you read *Pilgrim's Progress*? Perhaps it should be like that. What was Candide after? He wasn't after anything was he?
D : Yes he was. He was after the Princess. That was why he was kicked out in the first place. When he gets her she's hideous and covered with V.D. But he is still in love with her. But you couldn't stage that to make it believable. It's just a literary device.
L : You could stage it. You'd just have to turn the whole thing over, and stand back from it, and make the endings a comment on the action—an alienation.
D : I suppose so.
Lindsay grins. Does he really believe what he's said?
D : Mind you, in *Amerika* the hero isn't after anything. He just gets shoved to and fro suffering injustice.
L : That's true. I mean our character—perhaps he should just want to be successful? I mean to make it epic, to give it an epic quality, a view of society, it ought to be quite separate things he tries, thinking each time that this is going to be marvellous, this is the answer, then when it collapses he tries something new—so each time we see a completely different section of life. That would be epic . . . I suppose you want a whisky?
D : Please.
L : Help yourself. By the way: what about that book *The Hand-*

reared Boy, what did you think of it? I mean you didn't react to it really did you? You don't really enthuse about anything do you?
D: Yes I do. I loved the book. I told you. But I thought it would be impossible to make.
L: But if it were made it would make a fortune.
D: Yes it would.
L: Then why, when you read it, didn't you say it was very exciting and would make a film? You didn't react at all.
D: When I read it I didn't look on it as a film. I just read it as an ordinary reader and I enjoyed it—as a normal reader.
L: A normal reader! You don't think I keep sending you these books for you to read as an ordinary reader? You're supposed to be one of the most sought-after script-writers in the country—you don't think I sent you stuff to enjoy as a normal person. You're not a normal person.
D: Yes, but when I read it I realised that it would be impossible to make into a film. I just enjoyed . . .
L: Why is it impossible?
D: How do you as a director use small children in direct sexual actions without perverting them and exploiting them?
L: And being sent to jail.
D: And rightly.
L: Yes that's what I thought. That's why I thought it was impossible. . . Well what are we going to call our film?
D: *Lucky Man*.
L: No. *O Lucky Man*, like *O Dreamland* or *Oh Calcutta! O Lucky Man*—much better than *Lucky Man*—it's got a ring to it—and it ought to have an exclamation mark—where should the exclamation mark go?
D: At the beginning. After the 'O'.
L: At the end. *O Lucky Man!*

2nd September, 1970
Malcolm and I meet Lindsay who is working at the Royal Court Theatre. We go to a coffee bar round the corner. We sit on high stools over weak coffee to finalise our plans to produce *O Lucky Man!* We have to form a Company to make and own the film. Lindsay wants to call it Manic Productions, but settles for SAM, based on our initials. The three of us will be paid an equal amount for the whole film, £10,000 and each will have an equal vote in any SAM decision. Democracy. We have all brought prototype contracts

from our prospective lawyers. We pull them out. One is bound in black tape, one green, one red. They are each biased in favour of their client and against the others. After having read the others' contracts we decide to amalgamate them into one master contract so as to be fair to all. This we do with Lindsay's red Tempo pen. We cross everything out that we don't like in each other's contract —initialling every crossing out: 3 sets of initials for every crossing out or insertion. It takes 45 minutes. So SAM was born to produce its one and only film. We drink a toast to SAM in coffee.

20th September, 1970
Lindsay, Malcolm and I walk through the Inns of Court, looking for Lindsay's lawyer's office. We get lost in the Oxford-College-like quadrangles. It starts to rain heavily. We arrive ten minutes late, and drenched, to find a room full of expectant lawyers, and Lindsay's and Malcolm's agents. . .
It is apparent at this meeting that these people have different objectives from ours—of setting up the film simply, without a big, unnecessary, financial hassle. They are driven to complicate things as much as possible. This creates work for themselves. . .
Lindsay tells them we aren't interested and we must keep it simple. . . The meeting lasts an hour and a half. "It was like directing a film", Lindsay says afterwards, "The amount of energy you need to cut your way through the financial and legal snares—if we go on this way we'll be too exhausted to make the picture."
But, coming out of the Inns of Court, we feel like millionaires, after all the talk about percentages and profits. Unfortunately nothing concrete has been decided; we don't have a producer: we don't have a frame of film to our name, only 3 pages of script (*the car crash scene; the only scene in the story to remain unaltered through the $2\frac{1}{2}$ years of making the film*); no one has yet put up any money, and we don't have a deal with any major distributor.

We decide to go ahead with our development of our script without the backing—and the consequent sense of obligation—of a distributor. This was how I had developed *If*. . . . with Lindsay; and we felt freer that way. We also decide to wait until we have a reasonable first draft before approaching a producer. Malcolm and Lindsay each put up a modest stake and I put up my services as writer. (The only stake I had). So we got going.

26th February, 1971
Lindsay and I drive to Liverpool to inspect the actual coffee factory, where Malcolm trained as a coffee salesman. We find it very different from the factory Malcolm had described. It has shrunk. It is much too small. There are only four women on the packing lines.

A foreman, in a white linen pork-pie hat, shows us around. He explains the intricacies of roasting, blending, gas-flushing, and why although tea-bags have revolutionised the tea industry, coffee in similar bags would be flat as a flute. I take down pages of notes which I compress into a 3 page scene in which the foreman lectures the trainees...

We drive on north towards Bolton to visit Alan Price, where he is doing a gig with Georgie Fame. He is staying at Dimple Hall, an isolated stone farmhouse... It is Alan's regular lodging place when he is on a Northern tour. Everything is uncannily quiet. Late that evening we go with Alan, Georgie Fame and their group to Bolton where they are to give a concert. We drive to the gig, huddled in their freezing van.

Our night drives in this van later gave us the idea that the musicians' van should rescue our hero, Mick, when he is fleeing from the experimental medical laboratory.

The concert takes place in a nightclub unlike anything to be found in the south. It is huge, modern, densely packed; standing room only. The crowds of smartly dressed workers are in darkness. Only the stage is spotlit. Alan and Georgie sing their hit songs—*Simon Smith, Bonnie and Clyde,* and the rest as well as rock and rhythm and blues classics. Lindsay and I take photographs. After the concert the musicians unwind at Dimple Hall by playing Scrabble until four in the morning. Lindsay and I lose every game.

Lindsay had been planning a film with and about Alan Price after Alan had written the music for *Home*. It was to be a documentary, featuring gigs, travel, digs and one-night stands. Like the old actor-managers with their travelling fitups. But when Alan teamed up with Georgie Fame the project ran into difficulties, chiefly on copyright for the material they were using. (£1,000 a minute for a Ray Charles number). But quite a lot of the idea became part of *O Lucky Man!*

"Alan's songs—they're the one thing that will save this film," Lindsay says, after Alan has written My Home Town, Poor People,

Everyone's Going Through Changes, O Lucky Man! *and* Sell, Sell, Sell.

28th February, 1971
We spend two nights watching Alan Price and Georgie Fame, then drive back south to London. On the drive we discuss the scene when Mick meets the big-business man. Something else is needed in this scene, says Lindsay, something that will tell us the business man's power, the way he operates. I suggest a mad inventor who is given the boot. Kicked out after 40 years' service on which the company's fortune is based. Lindsay likes the idea. He thinks the inventor should commit suicide in front of Mick and the business man's eyes —hurl himself through the window at the top of Centrepoint.
This business-man became Sir James—father of a girl—Patricia— whom Mick meets in the musicians' van...

... To help me make a start in the research of 'Sir James', Malcolm rang the Chairman of E.M.I., Sir Joseph Lockwood, whom he had met while making the film, The Raging Moon, *for EMI. Sir Joseph Lockwood agreed to explain to us some of the mysteries of big business...*

5th July, 1971
Malcolm and I drive in his car to the E.M.I. Headquarters in Manchester Square. Sir Joseph Lockwood sees us in his huge boardroom. He tells us some of the truths of business : —
"The pioneer always pays," he says. "The first invention—no one wants to know. Look at tape cassettes."
We ask him how he chooses an employee?
"What has he done so far? Once he's past 30, degrees don't mean a thing. So long as he can read and write. If you've had failure you'll go on being a failure. If you've had success—you'll go on having success. Unless you go gaga. First thing a successful man in business has got to do is get rid of non-essentials. Never make wrong decisions... Good health. Sleep well. You should like to make money but not to spend it, unless it's going to make more money. Don't go off at the weekend. No round the world trips with the wife. It's not a question of morals—not morals—it's waste. Once you allow waste it goes right down the company. You end up ruined, be you the United States or a fish and chip shop at the Battersea Fun Fair."

I used this speech in the script—spoken by Sir James to Mick in the back of his Rolls Royce. It was shot, but all cut out in the editing.

. . . In the last quarter of the story Mick meets the poor. I visited Release, Shelter, and the Simon Community several times and laboured long at scenes involving Mick, social workers, and the destitute. . .

. . . All this research proved to be in the wrong direction. The naturalism of the social-worker scenes was too low-key, too straight. The style of the film needed continual heightening—the note of satire. Lindsay only fully realised this the day before he was due to shoot these scenes. It was mid-May, 1972. He rang me at 2 a.m.: "The Community Centre scenes are absolutely wrong. They won't work. I'll have to stop the film—unless you're on the set at 9 a.m. with a solution".
I arrived at 9 a.m. to find a large room at Colet Court redressed as a Community Centre and filled with old-age pensioners waiting to do their scene. Went up to the chilly production office. "Well?" asked Lindsay. "Cut it. Cut the whole thing," I said. To my surprise Lindsay agreed with relief: "Now you'll just have to find a brand new invention to put in its place. Got your typewriter?"

31st July, 1971
Go down on the train with Lindsay to Hythe—to spend the weekend working. On the train he reads the first draft for the first time, groaning and closing his eyes.
"It's terrible," he says.
Then he comes to three blank pages.
"What's this?"
"It's the scene on the roof. Mick and the girl. It's a complete blank —I can't think of anything. It's totally unreal. I can't write it."
"You'll just have to this weekend or we'll have to pack in the film."
Lindsay has booked into a three star hotel on the sea front where his mother is staying. I'm booked into a no-star hotel behind it. It is occupied mainly by permanent guests : old age pensioners who have made the cold little rooms into their final nests. As I walk down the long linoed corridor I can see into one of the rooms—it's crammed with potted plants, the dressing table crowded with framed photos of the owner's family. In the hall a gong with a floor brush hanging beside it which serves as a hammer.

There's no table in my room so I set the typewriter on the chair by the bed. But feel so depressed about the script, and the unwritable scene on the roof, that I go to the nearest pub. Drink and read the *Daily Mirror* over and over.
That evening Lindsay phones Malcolm.
"The author's lying drunk on the floor and the script is in ruins. You'd better meet me at the flat on Monday—I think we'll have to seriously consider forgetting the whole idea."
Malcolm mumbles "Oh God, I'll never work again."
Lindsay says to me—"Write that roof top scene tomorrow morning."
"It's a complete blank. Nothing there."
"Just write something. Anything you like."
I go back to my hotel. It is 10.30 p.m. Not a light in the place. Everyone is in their own room, trying to sleep.

2nd August, 1971
I wake up to the sound of the gong being beaten with the brush. I run down to breakfast. About ten very aged guests gathered at the same table shouting into each other's hearing aids; I'm put at a table by myself, away from them; in the far corner also set on her own, is a beautiful Arab girl. Why should she choose this hotel? Anyway, feel cheered up. Buy newspaper and go upstairs to read about the Oz trial. Lock the door in case Lindsay should make one of his unannounced inspections and find me reading the newspaper and the typewriter silent. Put down paper and write first line—he said write anything : very well. . .
Later Lindsay phones Malcolm again and says—"Author woke up in the morning and produced some very good work in the afternoon."
Malcolm says—"I know it will be good. Just keep him off the Barley Wine."
Alan Price had once told Lindsay about staying in a big hotel when he was playing a gig in Lancashire, and the hotel manager had invited him to an orgy in a shed behind the hotel. It seemed a good idea for Mick, after his first unsuccessful day on the road trying to sell coffee, to end up in a similar situation.

18th August, 1971
Writing in the office in Lindsay's flat. Another blank in the script— the orgy scene in the Yorkshire Hotel. At 9.30 a.m. I tell Lindsay

it's impossible to write and we'll have to think of a completely different invention.
"I've got a shock for you, Malcolm's coming in at 11 a.m. and I've promised him he can read the orgy."
"But I've never been to an orgy."
"Perhaps it should be like the other orgy Alan told me about. He was in the North of England and he looked through the window of this respectable suburban house and saw the head of police, and the mayor, and all their wives—just sitting—watching blue films."
"All right. Hmm. . . Why is it I never get asked to orgies?"
"Because you don't look sporty enough."
I decide that the key to the orgy must be respectability and good-neighbourliness. Mick being introduced to everyone as though it were a vicarage jumble-sale. Finish it just in time. The absolute necessity of having a deadline, however artificial.

September, 1971
Lindsay went to Czechoslovakia. He had to get permission for Mirek Ondricek, the cameraman who had shot If. . . . *to visit England to shoot* O Lucky Man! *He spent a very frustrating week in Prague, everybody very friendly, but difficult to get a definite 'yes'. When he came back he rang me:*
"How much have you written?"
"Just a bit."
"Just a bit?! That's absolutely useless."
He slammed the phone down. Half an hour later he rang back. We both laugh. Conversation continues as if uninterrupted. He thinks they will let Mirek come.

Late September, 1971
Getting the script together:
I am going mad trying to finish the scene in the musicians' van when Mick meets Patricia; 7 people in a small van—each movement has to be clearly worked out in relation to the size of the van, the dramatic states of the characters, and the actual distance travelled during the journey. Lindsay lends me some tapes he made with Alan Price in his van, but I can't hear a word because of the engine noise and the broadness of Alan's Newcastle accent. I phone Malcolm for ideas, but he was off to record his commentary for The Clockwork Orange. *Lindsay was also going mad trying to cast* The Changing Room. *He had to find 15 Northern actors who*

looked as though they could all be members of the same Rugby League team. He was absolutely exhausted.
There was now a plethora of drafts for some scenes, which had to be synthesised into one. In the evenings and at weekends, when Lindsay was not working at The Royal Court, we would take it in turns dictating from the almost illegible scrawled-over, earlier drafts, while the other typed out the finalised version. We drink a lot of Barley Wine.

15th October, 1971
First draft completed.
After finishing the first draft we showed it to Michael Medwin, as we had done with If. . . . He understood it immediately, liked it immediately, and agreed to join us as producer. Old collaborators were contacted. Many of them knew about the project already: Miroslav Ondricek, our Cameraman; Jocelyn Herbert, Production Designer; Miriam Brickman, Casting; David Gladwell, Editor. . . Michael started contacting distributors for finance. From the start Warner Brothers were the keenest. British Finance, as before, was not forthcoming.

24th December, 1971
A postcard from New York; a painting of two hamburgers. On the other side is written in red Tempo :
'Dec 21st—Concluded deal with Warner Bros at 9 p.m. Budget 1.5 million dollars. All we have to do now is make the film. Happy Xmas. Love Lindsay.'

Sunday 19th March, 1972
The day before shooting starts. At Lindsay's flat, still trying to rewrite the roof top scene for the eighth time. Malcolm rings Lindsay—"I've got to see you immediately. I don't understand a word of this script."
Malcolm arrives. He thinks the character is a sheep, too passive. I tell him all the best actors are passive. They react. Look at Robert Mitchum. This is a reacting part.
"But he needs a bit more go—don't you think?"
"Well you re-write it then. By tomorrow," says Lindsay.
"Listen you've got to pretend to be naive," he says "it's how you were ten years ago. Go on now—you've just got to do it."
So Malcolm went away, content.

23rd March, 1972
Third day of shooting. I go to the set—the location is a coffee factory in South London. It is a sunny, suddenly hot day. Outside the factory stand generating lorries for our lights. Inside the factory the skylights have been covered with tarpaulins to keep out the unexpected sun. Blocks of lamps hanging in the ceiling behind translucent paper seem to provide exactly the same effect as the sunlight. The camera dominates everything. It is mounted high on a wooden scaffold at the far end of the factory floor.

I make myself inconspicuous next to a coffee packing machine and read through, for the nth time, the rewrite of the rewrite of the roof-top scene. The detached ruthless attitude of the girl, Patricia, is still not there. I look at the coffee packing lines away from the shooting area. They are working normally, but all the packers wear red badges on their uniforms, reading 'Imperial Coffee' instead of their own brand.

Lindsay, Malcolm and Arthur Lowe stand under the blaze of light, surrounded by boxes of coffee. Mirek, the director of photography lines up the shot on the scaffold. Lindsay suddenly puts his hand on Arthur Lowe's shoulder to draw his attention. Lindsay points an accusing finger straight at me.

"Him—the author . . . he's to blame."

Credits

Screenplay by	David Sherwin
based on an idea by	Malcolm McDowell
Directed by	Lindsay Anderson
Produced by	Michael Medwin & Lindsay Anderson
Production Company	Memorial-SAM
Music and Songs	Alan Price
Production Designer	Jocelyn Herbert
Director of Photography	Miroslav Ondricek
Editor	David Gladwell
Supervising Editor	Tom Priestley
Associate Producer	Basil Keys
Art Director	Alan Withy
Assistant Director	Derek Cracknell
Sound Recordist	Chris Wangler
Camera Operator	Herbert Smith
Gaffer	Len Crowe
Second Assistant	Richard Jenkins
Production Manager	Don Toms
Sound Editor	Alan Bell
Dubbing Mixer	Doug Turner
Assistant Editors	Neil Thomson
	Michael Ellis
Associate Art Director	Ted Marshall
Special Effects	John Stears
Set Decorator	Harry Cordwell
Construction	Jack Carter
Casting	Miriam Brickman

Continuity	Valerie Booth
Wardrobe	Elsa Fennell
Hairdresser	Colin Jamison
Make-up	Paul Rabiger, Basil Newall
Made on location in	England and Scotland
Distributed by	Warner Bros Inc

Malcolm McDowell	Mick
Ralph Richardson	Monty
	Sir James
Rachel Roberts	Gloria Rowe
	Madame Paillard
	Mrs Richards
Arthur Lowe	Mr Duff
	Charlie Johnson
	Dr Munda
Helen Mirren	Patricia
Graham Crowden	Professor Millar
	Professor Stewart
	Meths Drinker
Peter Jeffrey	Factory Chairman
	Prison Governor
Dandy Nichols	Tea Lady
	Neighbour
Mona Washbourne	Sister Hallett
	Usher
	Neighbour
Philip Stone	Interrogator
	Jenkins
	Salvation Army Major
Mary Macleod	Mary Ball
	Vicar's Wife
	Salvationist
Michael Bangerter	Interrogator
	William
	Released Prisoner
	Assistant
Wallas Eaton	John Stone
	Colonel Steiger
	Warder

	Meths Drinker
	Film Executive
Warren Clarke	Master of Ceremonies
	Male Nurse
	Warner
Bill Owen	Superintendent Barlow
	Inspector Carding
Edward Judd	Oswald
Pearl Nunez	Mrs Naidu
Geoffrey Palmer	Doctor
	Basil Keyes
Michael Medwin	Army Captain
	Power Station Technician
	Duke of Belminster
Vivian Pickles	Good Lady
Geoffrey Chater	Vicar
	Bishop
Anthony Nicholls	General
	Judge
Brian Glover	Foreman
	Power Station Guard
Jeremy Bulloch	Young Man
	Pig-Boy
David Baker, Edward Peel	Policemen
Alan Price	Alan
Colin Greene	Colin (Guitar)
Ian Leake	Roadie
Clive Thacker	Clive (Drums)
Dave Markee	Dave (Bass Guitar)

With : Bart Alison, Ben Aris, John Barrett, Margot Bennett, James Bolam, Sue Bond, Constance Chapman, Peter Childs, Frank Cousins, Brian Croucher, Allen Cullen, Paul Dawkins, Anna Dawson, Michael Elphick, Eleanor Fazan, Pat Healey, Geoff Hinsliff, Jo Jeggo, Patricia Lawrence, Stephanie Lawrence, Brian Lawson, Terence Maidment, Tuesday Miller, Christine Noonan, Ken Oxtoby, Stuart Perry, Brian Pettifer, Bill Pilkington, Cyril Renison, Irene Richmond, Roy Scammell, Peter Schofield, Frank Singuineau, Patsy Smart, David Stern, Adele Strong, Hugh Thomas, Betty Turner, Glenn Williams, Catherine Willmer

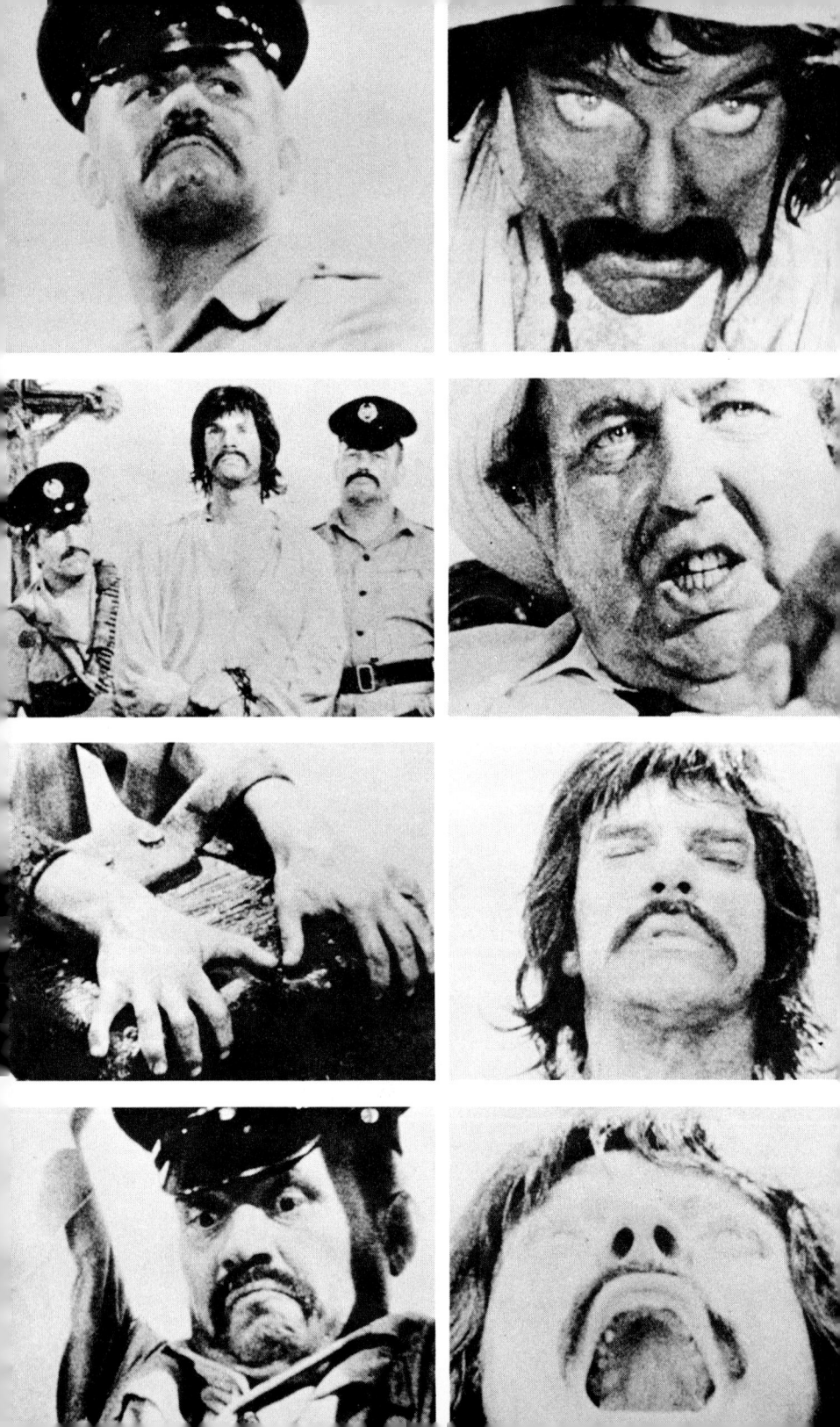

O Lucky Man!

PROLOGUE

TITLE: *ONCE UPON A TIME*

COFFEE PLANTATION

Iris out from a PEASANT to a series of images in the style of a silent Russian film.
Peasants in wide straw hats are bent double as they move along lines of coffee plants, picking the beans. An armed FOREMAN, hard-faced, walks between the lines of peasants, pushing them roughly aside. He carries a gun at the ready. Another armed GUARD watches over them.
A PEASANT fills his sack with beans.

TITLE: *COFFEE FOR THE BREAKFAST TABLE*

Coffee beans are poured from a sack into a basket.
A PEASANT picks beans, watched over by an armed GUARD.
The armed FOREMAN's boots crush the soil as he walks.
He pushes a PEASANT aside with his stick.
A beautiful GIRL picking beans looks up at the FOREMAN, apprehensively.
The FOREMAN, bull-necked, surveys the pickers.
A gaunt PEASANT is stealing beans. He slips them into a bag inside his shirt.
The FOREMAN is watching him.

TITLE: *UNLUCKY*

The gaunt PEASANT's face. He looks up fearfully.
The FOREMAN looks down at him, grimly smiling.

TITLE : *JUSTICE*

A Coat of Arms. Beneath it sits a JUDGE, unshaven and filthy. He is slumped in a chair, smoking a cigar.
The gaunt PEASANT stands guarded in the dock. A crucifix on the wall behind him. His hands are chained.
His weeping wife and children (a girl and a boy, aged three or four) watch from the gallery.
The PEASANT stands guarded in the dock.
The JUDGE removes the cigar from his fat lips. Saliva runs down his chin. He points at the prisoner, and mouths the word 'Guilty'.

TITLE : *'GUILTY!'*

The PEASANT's eyes widen in terror.

TITLE : *'GUILTY!'*

The JUDGE's mouth, huge, pronounces the word.

TITLE : *'GUILTY!'*

The FOREMAN's hands draw a heavy machette from his belt. They grasp the weapon.
The PEASANT stares up, wide-eyed.
The FOREMAN looks menacingly down at the PEASANT, then lowers the machette and runs its sharp edge over his wrists.
He raises his weapon up, back, over his head.
The PEASANT prepares himself, tensing. His hands are strapped to a block.
The FOREMAN glances away, as if for a signal. He swings his weapon down with sudden violent force.
The PEASANT's head jerks back. His mouth opens in a scream.
BLACKOUT

TITLE : *NOW*

CREDIT SEQUENCE

LIMBO
Hands strike a piano keyboard.
In a Limbo setting—black curtains encircling a central space—ALAN PRICE and his group of three musicians play the song

O Lucky Man! ALAN, seated at his electric piano, plays and sings. Grouped in a circle before him are COLIN on guitar, DAVE on bass, and TOLLY on drums. Outside the circle film technicians can be seen from time to time: the DIRECTOR in scarlet shirt and leather jacket, the continuity girl taking notes, the cameraman shooting with a hand-held Arriflex, the assistant director drinking beer. Tables are littered with glasses and bottles of Newcastle Brown. Two large mirrors and two or three posters are hanging on the black curtains. The atmosphere is smoky, concentrated, relaxed, like a good rehearsal run-through. The group is casually, not fashionably or eccentrically, dressed.

ALAN (singing):
>*If you have a friend on whom you think you can rely—*
>>*You are a lucky man!*
>*If you've found the reason to live and not to die—*
>>*You are a lucky man!*
>*Preachers and poets and scholars don't know it,*
>*Temples and statues and steeples won't show it,*
>*If you've got the secret just try not to blow it—*
>>*Stay a lucky man!*

> *If you've found the meaning of the truth in this old*
> *world—*
> *You are a lucky man!*
> *If knowledge hangs around your neck like pearls instead*
> *of chains—*
> *You are a lucky man!*
> *Takers and fakers and talkers won't tell you,*
> *Teachers and preachers will just buy and sell you,*
> *When no one can tempt you with heaven or hell—*
> *You'll be a lucky man!*
>
> *You'll be better by far*
> *To be just what you are—*
> *You can be what you want*
> *If you are what you are*
> *—and that's a lucky man!*

During the song the DIRECTOR rises, crosses to ALAN while he is still playing, checks the lyric with him. In the background the camera is seen tracking round, the CAMERA ASSISTANT with his hand on the focus control, a PROP MAN fanning smoke into the playing area.

BLACKOUT

TITLE: *WEST*

MOTORWAY FLYOVER

The camera tracks along a busy motorway. Looking sideways we see the roofs and huge factory buildings of an industrial estate. A sign on one of these factories reads: 'IMPERIAL COFFEE.' The sound track fills with the clattering, echoing, humming noises of a busy manufacturing plant.

THE COFFEE FACTORY

A sign hangs inside the factory: 'AUTOMATIC ROASTING SECTION.' The camera tracks past the sign to an overhead view of a large, vibrating machine. This is an all-purpose giant (apocryphal) into which is blown, through a bulky circular duct, a flow of raw coffee beans. Steel handles, dials and gauges ornament the front of the machine. A round plate-glass door high up in the centre shows the raw material whirling around within.

Five or six trainee salesmen in white linen coats and wearing white linen pork-pie hats troop in to confront this machine listening, with varying degrees of attention, to a technical description by JOHN STONE, the foreman of the section. They carry clipboards.

JOHN STONE is earnest, with a rather high-pitched voice. The trainees are: MR GREASY, in his thirties, an ex-insurance salesman; MACINTYRE, about 35, an ex-army Captain; SPALDING, thin and nervous; BILES in his early twenties, spotty, long-haired and just out of technical college. The brightest of them is MICHAEL TRAVIS, also in his early twenties. He is alert, energetic and quickly bored. He has great ambition and a considerable gift of fantasy—it would need no great effort of imagination for him to see himself, for instance, as Chairman of Imperial Coffee. He is very sincere, but there is not yet a great depth to his sincerity. He was expelled from school for insubordination.

The trainees listen to JOHN STONE. He speaks to them against the noise of the machinery. No one can understand a word.

JOHN STONE leads the trainees to another part of the machine.

As he talks on, MICK eyes the women working on the packing lines nearby. One is young, working automatically, chattering and laughing as she works.

JOHN STONE leads the trainees to another part of the shop floor. In single file they troop down the end of a loading bay. As they come past the packing section MICK breaks away, dodging under the conveyor, up to the GIRL he has already spotted.

MICK: Hello.
GIRL: Hello.
MICK: Do you realise this Nigerian Coffee is being packed straight back to Nigeria?
GIRL (giggling): Frightening isn't it?

The GIRL slaps a pack of coffee into his outstretched hand.

MICK: Been here long?
JOHN STONE (shouting): Mr Travis—Mr Travis!
MICK: See you.

MICK prances off to join the other trainees gathered round the large packing machine. It is quieter here.

JOHN STONE: This Hesser is our latest machine. It gives a four-sided seal and runs 72 packs a minute.

    A woman is testing and weighing the packs. JOHN STONE tears a pack open and pours the coffee from the torn pack into a half-full bin of ground coffee.

JOHN STONE: Any fault in the plastic packing can cause a break. The coffee is now returned to our patent coffee processor. Why is that Mr Biles?

    BILES looks up nervously.

BILES: I've been off sick, sir.

MICK (brightly): Eliminates waste, sir.

MR DUFF (off-screen): Absolutely correct!

    The trainees turn to see that MR DUFF, the Works Manager, has joined them. A brisk man, conscious of his position and responsibility. He wears a brown suit—no white coat or hat.

    JOHN STONE immediately shows deference.

MR DUFF (continuing): Always remember, gentlemen, that you're a failure in catering if you don't know what to do with your leftovers. Right—I'll take them off your hands now, Mr Stone. Follow me, gentlemen.

    He leads them off. The woman continues to weigh her packs.
BLACKOUT

LECTURE HALL
A moderate-sized room arranged like a lecture hall or science lab. Four rows of desks in rising tiers look down on a space where there is a table and chair. On the table: a telephone, vase of flowers, pad of clean paper, pencils, etc. Beside it another chair on which is sitting GLORIA ROWE, the firm's Public Relations Officer, poised, blonde and shrewd.

MR DUFF has taken off his watch and put it on the table. He addresses the trainees as they sit.

MR DUFF: Now gentlemen you have learned the Number One truth—that a cup of Imperial Coffee is the only proper way to finish a meal, be it in a palace or a prison.

The trainees try to take in MR DUFF'S words.

MR DUFF: But between the making and the drinking must stand the salesmen. And this is where you come in. You will be our representatives in the front line. Each one of you is going to have to prove himself on the battlefield of Sales. It's a hard road you have to travel. There will be whole days when you won't sell a bean. But you'll go out the very next day and hit the jackpot.

MICK puts up his hand.

MICK: Mr Duff—may I ask a question?

MR DUFF: Certainly, Mr Travers.

MICK: Travis.

MR DUFF: I beg your pardon.

MICK: How much does a top salesman get paid?

MICK has caught the attention of GLORIA.

MR DUFF: Of course—your basic salary will be low—£11.50 per week before tax. But for a good man, with commission, the sky's the limit. Our star salesman at the moment—a wonderful man called Jim Oswald takes home anything from £75 to £150 per week.

As MR DUFF continues, we see MICK'S hand carefully inscribing in large figures on his clipboard pad. BILES peers to see.

£150
52
———
7,500
300
———
£7,800

MR DUFF: Now I've never lied to you, never given you false hopes.

But I believe in you. With a coffee pack in one hand and your sales list in the other—I want you to be one long line of shining success. From John O'Groats to Land's End. (Mr Duff puts his watch back on and gathers his papers.) Now selling is psychology. A good salesman must know something about psychology. And in that particular field I can think of no better authority than our Chief of Public Relations—Mrs Gloria Rowe.

    Gloria rises and comes to the centre as Mr Duff sits. For a moment she holds the trainees with a steady gaze. Then she speaks.

Gloria : Mr Spalding, please.

    Spalding shifts uneasily.

Gloria : Come here, Mr Spalding.

    Spalding stands and shuffles clumsily to the front. He stands awkwardly before Gloria.

Gloria : Smile.

    Gloria approaches Spalding, who seems mesmerised, and shakes his hand.

Gloria : *Smile,* Mr Spalding.

    Gloria smiles at Spalding, deeply, warmly. He makes a tentative grimace. Duff bows his head in despair. Gloria turns briskly, discarding Spalding, and speaks to the trainees.

Gloria : Imperial product is good. But people don't buy things just because they're good. They have to believe. And you have to inspire that belief . . . You have to believe. Remember the words of William Blake : 'A sincere belief that anything is so will make it so.' Sincerity. Honesty.

    Mick receives these words with candour, innocence. Gloria calls :

Gloria : Mr Macintyre, Mr Travis, Mr Greasy! Thank you, Mr Spalding.

Spalding : Thank you.

    The three trainees stand up and make their way forward. Gloria singles out Mr Macintyre first.

Gloria : Hello, Mr Macintyre!

    She moves towards him, extending her hand. He takes it nervously.

Gloria : Smile. Give with all your heart. Don't think of yourself. Relax those cheek muscles.

    She takes his cheeks with her hands, forcing his mouth into a grotesque smile.

GLORIA: Smile, Mr Macintyre!
  But it is useless. GLORIA turns her attention to MICK.
GLORIA: Mr Travis.
  MICK steps forward briskly, with confidence.
MICK: Morning, Mrs Rowe.
  MICK's smile is radiant. GLORIA turns, like an astronomer who has discovered a new star, to address the other trainees.
GLORIA: Now that is sincerity. That is a completely sincere smile. ... If I was a buyer and these were two travellers, I'd definitely buy from the guy I like. I'd definitely buy from the sincere personality. I'm definitely going to buy from you, Mr Travis.
  The phone rings, and MR DUFF answers it. GLORIA continues.
MR DUFF: Lecture Hall here. Duff speaking.
GLORIA: Now, Mr Travis I want you to smile at Mr Greasy. Mr Greasy, smile back and give Mr Travis a firm handshake.
  GREASY stretches out his hand and MICK grasps it. MR DUFF rises, finishing off his phone conversation.
MR DUFF: Certainly, Chairman. Of course. Right away.
GLORIA (taking Greasy's hand): Mr Greasy, don't think I'm being personal, but when we're dealing with food products, 'hygiene' must

be our motto. Make sure you've got clean fingernails.
MR DUFF (coming forward into the group): Mrs Rowe . . . The Chairman wants to see us immediately. . . . Take a break, gentlemen. I'll see you on the shop floor in twenty minutes.
DUFF and GLORIA make briskly for the door.
BLACKOUT

THE CHAIRMAN'S OFFICE
A panelled office, dominated by a heavy mahogany desk. Behind it an oil painting of a dark-skinned tribal woman carrying a large basket of coffee on her head. The CHAIRMAN, handsomely middle-aged, is at the desk towering over his executives. His face is grave. GLORIA and MR DUFF are sitting in chairs in front of his desk, as well as two other executives behind them.
CHAIRMAN: Gentlemen, I have very bad news. Oswald has left the North-East.
A stunned pause. Serious looks of concern.
MR DUFF (in shock): Left? . . .
CHAIRMAN: Vanished. Disappeared. No notice. Nothing. Just one ruddy great hole on the map. And that's not all. Oswald is suspected of trafficking in stolen goods under Imperial's name.
EXECUTIVES: Oh my God! . . . Great Scot!
CHAIRMAN: Well, I need an immediate replacement. Mr Duff, how are your trainees?
The CHAIRMAN moves to a window set in the wall of his room. He slides it open. Factory noise floods in. This window looks down on the shop floor.
MR DUFF: They're very good, sir. But they need another two weeks.
CHAIRMAN: No. No—I can't wait . . . Mrs Rowe.
He beckons her over. GLORIA rises and he puts his arm around her. Together they stand looking down on the floor.
CHAIRMAN (to GLORIA): Now what's your instinct say?
The trainees are there with cups of tea in their hands by the tea trolley, the tea lady dispenses tea and biscuits. MICK has strolled away from the group of trainees. He is about to chat up the GIRL on the Assembly Line.
GLORIA and the CHAIRMAN continue looking.
CHAIRMAN: Who's my man? Can you sniff him?
MICK turns and looks up at GLORIA and the CHAIRMAN.
GLORIA draws the CHAIRMAN's attention to MICK.

MICK smiles—the Smile.
GLORIA: Travis. That's your man.
BLACKOUT

THE CHAIRMAN'S OFFICE
MICK, now in a brown suit and neatly brushed hair, is sitting to attention in front of the CHAIRMAN's desk. He looks at the CHAIRMAN steadily. GLORIA is sitting to the side, all awareness and discretion. The CHAIRMAN speaks with gravity.
CHAIRMAN: Travis, we're in a jam. You've heard about Oswald. It's a case of all hands to the pumps.
MICK: I understand, sir.
CHAIRMAN: Now Mrs Rowe has spoken highly of you, and I've never known her wrong. So I'm going to play her hunch. I'm giving you the North-East.
A brief pause for effect . . . then the CHAIRMAN rises momentously and walks to the side of the picture behind his desk. As he presses a button, we see that it is painted on strips: these revolve to show a map of England, divided boldly into sales areas. He points to the map. MICK, earnest, looks on.
CHAIRMAN: Now that's as far North as the Border; as far West as Lancashire; and as far South as the Humber. It's a big challenge. Do you think you're up to it?
MICK: I know I am, sir.
CHAIRMAN: Normally an opportunity like this wouldn't come your way for ten or twenty years. Men far more experienced than you have had their shot at it and been broken by it. But you've got guts and you've got ambition. And that gives you a head start. Good luck.
MICK rises and comes forward to the desk. The CHAIRMAN shakes him by the hand and then hands him his talismans.
CHAIRMAN: Now, here is your card: never travel without it. Your map, your compass, and your car keys. Now go out there and fight.
MICK: I will, sir. Every inch of the way. You can rely on me.
MICK smiles.
CHAIRMAN: Good man. (MICK turns to go): He's all yours now, Mrs Rowe. Oh, and Travis . . .
The CHAIRMAN takes a green apple from a bowl on his desk and holds it out to MICK.
MICK (huskily): Thank you very much, sir.
MICK takes the apple, then turns away and leaves with GLORIA.

BLACKOUT

The CHAIRMAN takes another apple from the bowl, and bites firmly into it.
BLACKOUT

GLORIA ROWE'S OFFICE
An executive's office with the feminine touch. On a table three Conas are boiling and bubbling on an electric plate, with three cups in front of them.
GLORIA has changed into something soft, flowing and orange. . . . She spoons sugar into the cups.

GLORIA: Come here, Mr Travis. I'm going to give you a simple test . . .

MICK comes over as she pours coffee from a Cona into one of the cups.

GLORIA: . . . Be very careful how you answer. I want you to taste these cups of coffee. . . .

She pours coffee from the second cona into the second cup, and then from the third Cona into the third cup. This cup she

gives to MICK.
GLORIA : ... And tell me what they do for you.
MICK sips it carefully, smacking his lips expertly.
MICK : Sturdy ... plebeian ... . plenty of body ... a vigorous Robusta ... ?
GLORIA takes the cup from him and sniffs it.
GLORIA : Spicy ...
She puts the cup down and takes the second cup.
GLORIA : Now this ...
She tilts her head back and tastes the coffee, puckering her lips, delicately. She draws close to MICK and slowly puts her mouth against his. She transfers the coffee into his mouth. He swallows and it runs down his chin. She draws back and takes another sip of coffee. This time MICK comes to her : he drinks from her mouth. 'Glug, glug' noises as he drinks. MICK kisses her.
GLORIA : The future is in your hands, Mr Travis. Take it now.
MICK takes her. They sink together to the floor. The camera sinks half-way with them, to hold the bubbling Conas. The bubbling of the Conas gives way to the soft rattle of maracas.

LIMBO
The group again—we first see them in the large mirror suspended against the black surround. They play the song *Poor People*. The camera pans down and across the dark space to confront ALAN as he sings. Listening to the music are two or three bystanders—including the ROADIE and PATRICIA, a girl in her early twenties with long fair hair and a flowing dress. The camera circles the group, then pans away into the dark.
ALAN (singing) : *Poor people are poor people*
They don't understand
A man's got to make whatever he wants—
Take it with his own hands.

Poor people stay poor people—
They never get to see
Someone's got to win in the human race—
If it isn't you then it has to be me.

So smile while you're making it—
Laugh while you're taking it—
Even though you're faking it—
Nobody's gonna know.

It's no use mumbling,
It's no use grumbling,
Life just isn't fair—
No easy days
No easy ways
Just get out there
And do it!

So sing and they'll sing your song—
Laugh while you're getting on—
Smile and they'll string along—
Nobody's gonna know.

THE PENNINE ROAD

MICK drives across the dales of Northern England, through the misty hills, in his clean Ford Anglia. The end of the song is heard on his transistor radio swinging above the dashboard. MICK changes the station, and the song mixes to the sound of a BBC announcer.

BBC ANNOUNCER: *. . . was commenting on the . . . and much of*

Central Southern England, though it probably won't reach the East Midlands till after Midnight. Now for Eastern England, Central Northern England and North East England. A foggy start in most places and a mostly dull misty day with rain and drizzle at times. The outlook for tomorrow and Saturday: Dry but cold at night with frost in places and fairly widespread fog. And that's the end of the weather forecast. And finally overseas posting for Christmas—tomorrow parcels should be posted to Argentina, Iraq via Lebanon and Trinidad; letters should go to Malaya and Anzac FPOS. . . .

    MICK's car drives towards the camera, his headlights on as the mist thickens.

    A red sports car comes up from behind, blaring its horn to overtake MICK. It is driven by a YOUNG MAN wearing a check tweed cap and an old Cheltonian scarf. MICK beckons him on and the sports car draws alongside. They stare fixedly at each other for a moment, then the YOUNG MAN gives a broad smile and zooms ahead down the road into the mist. MICK drives on. Then through the fog, he hears the blare of a horn, the scream of a skid, a crash. He stops his car, gets out and runs ahead. The sports car has run into a big grocery van. The van is on

its side: the driver has been thrown through the windscreen and is dead. The van's load of groceries is strewn across the road.

From the smashed sports car (Austin Healey) the YOUNG MAN groans. MICK runs to the car. The YOUNG MAN falls out of the driver's seat into the passenger seat, blood flowing from a wound in his head. MICK rushes round to the side of the car where the young man has flopped.

YOUNG MAN (moaning): Tell my mother I'm all right ... It's her birthday.

MICK takes off his coat and tucks it under the YOUNG MAN's head. He hears the sound of a car braking and looks round. Two POLICE OFFICERS draw up in a white Police car. They get out. One crosses the road to MICK, while the other appraises the wrecked van. Groceries are strewn across the road.

FIRST POLICE OFFICER (to MICK): You the only witness?

MICK: Yes, I saw it. I can give you a statement.

FIRST POLICE OFFICER: Don't bother.

The SECOND POLICE OFFICER bends down and starts to pick groceries up from the road. He comes to join them.

SECOND POLICE OFFICER: No need to detain the gentleman.
The YOUNG MAN groans again.
YOUNG MAN: Tell my mother...
The FIRST POLICE OFFICER kneels down by him. MICK looks on. Suddenly the car radio in the sports car comes on of its own accord.
RADIO SONG: *Hold me close wherever we go* .....
MICK leans into the car and switches it off. The FIRST POLICE OFFICER, who has knelt down by the dying boy, gets up.
FIRST POLICE OFFICER: He's gone. Now—scarper.
MICK: But what about him?
FIRST POLICE OFFICER: Done for. Perforated kidneys.
The FIRST POLICE OFFICER turns away and starts inspecting the groceries scattered across the road.
MICK: It was his fault. He was driving too fast.
SECOND POLICE OFFICER: Oh, we can see what happened. We'll be witnesses—save you the trouble.
MICK: Oh it's no trouble. I can give you a statement.
FIRST POLICE OFFICER (holding a large yellow cheese in his hand): As far as we're concerned it's a private accident. No one else involved. Unless you give a statement.
SECOND POLICE OFFICER: Then our Chief Constable might find you're involved. He might bring charges against you. Using us as witnesses.
FIRST POLICE OFFICER: Our word against yours.
MICK looks from one officer to the other. He is catching on.
SECOND POLICE OFFICER: So on your way, chummy, unless you want booking for manslaughter.
The FIRST POLICE OFFICER hands MICK a large cheese.
FIRST POLICE OFFICER: Here you are . . . Fair do's.
MICK: Fair do's.
MICK goes back to his car. As he gets in he looks back. Then he drives off as the SECOND POLICEMAN waves him forward through the debris. The POLICE OFFICERS start loading groceries into the boot of their car.
BLACKOUT

CITY ROAD
Early evening. The road from MICK's point of view as he drives into the city. A news report is heard on the transistor radio.

NEWS REPORTER: *A report from our Belfast newsroom. Two gunmen fired seven shots in all, aimed it seems at the sentries on duty in the grounds of the General's large house which is heavily guarded by soldiers and security staff with dogs. Soldiers fired back and later found traces of blood, which led them to believe they'd hit one of the gunmen.*
BLACKOUT

The car passes shop windows in the city centre. The news continues.

NEWS REPORTER: *The Egyptian War Minister, General Sadek, has resigned. The move was seen as a reflection of the dissension in Egypt over the country's relationship with the Soviet Union.*
BLACKOUT

MICK drives down a dark street looking for his lodgings. He takes out a piece of paper and refers to an address written on the back of it. He looks about in the darkness. His transistor is still playing.

ANNOUNCER: *And tonight 'It's Your Line' on the subject of mental health—It's estimated that one in six women and one in nine men will enter hospital at least once in their lives because of mental illness. What are the causes of the steady increase in mental illness—can they be avoided? Are we spending enough care and money on the mentally sick and the mentally handicapped? Are they better treated in hospital or in their own homes and communities?*

The car turns off a tree-lined street into the forecourt of a large Victorian house. An illuminated board on the garden wall carries the legend: 'SUTHERLAND HOUSE PRIVATE HOTEL PROPRIETRESS: MRS MARY BALL. TEL: WAKELY 4726.' MICK parks in the forecourt, and gets out.

SUTHERLAND HOUSE
The front door opens. MARY BALL greets MICK.
MARY: Mr Travis?
MICK: Hello. Good evening.
MARY, pneumatic, limpid-eyed, welcoming, not young but not old, smiles and invites him in.
MARY: Come in.
MICK: Thank you.

THE HALL
MICK comes into the hall carrying his suitcase, his briefcase and his cheese. MARY closes the front door behind him. There is a desk, two or three doors leading off, a staircase with heavy wooden banisters, and a wall telephone.

MARY: I was getting quite worried about you. It can be a nasty drive over those moors. Still—here you are, safe and sound. (She calls): Bill!

BILL, the handyman, appears. He is lugubrious, in shirtsleeves.

MARY opens the guestbook, which is lying on the desk under a gong, a wooden brush hanging from the frame to serve as a striker.

MARY: Would you sign the book, please? (As he signs): You've missed supper but I'll do you something special. (A look between MARY and BILL): Bill—would you show Mr Travis to his room.

MICK: Thank you very much. Thank you.

MICK moves to follow BILL upstairs. MARY notices he is forgetting his cheese, hastens to give it to him. MICK starts to climb the stairs behind BILL. MARY follows him to the bottom of the stairs and calls up.

MARY: Oh Mr Travis—I'm afraid Mr Oswald left quite a lot behind. I've put it in one of the drawers. I didn't like to throw it out.
MICK: That's all right. I'll manage. Thank you.
    She smiles at him.
    BLACKOUT

    MICK'S BEDROOM
    The room, which is rather bare, is set in the eaves at the top of the house. There is linoleum on the floor with a rug or two, a gas fire with a coin-in-the-slot meter, a single bed, a wardrobe, a chest of drawers, with a mirror and a vase of flowers on it. A chair stands near the bed. In the corner is a basin with a mirror above it.
    MICK unwraps the apple that the CHAIRMAN gave him, polishes it on his jacket and takes a bite as he starts to unpack his case. He takes out a new white shirt in cellophane wrapping and puts it in a drawer of the chest. He opens the top two drawers, which are both empty. The bottom drawer is crammed with OSWALD's things: chest expanders, photographs, teddy bear, bottles and clothes. He tests the chest expanders then he holds up and inspects an old, striped football jersey. He looks round as a voice speaks from the door.
MONTY: So you're the new rabbit.
    At the door stands MONTY, bespectacled. He appraises MICK. He is an elderly figure, agelessly old, wearing a woollen dressing gown. He is both secret and inquisitive, keeping himself to himself, yet somehow managing to know everything that's going on. He is never surprised.
MONTY: You're the replacement are you?
MICK: Who are you?
MONTY: Oh I live here. (MONTY sits down on the chair): Don't let me hold you up.
    MICK throws down the football jersey and pulls out a packet of cigarettes.
MICK: Would you like a cigarette?
    MONTY takes a cigarette; he waits for a light. MICK produces a lighter from his pocket and lights it for him. MICK continues to unpack from his suitcase. He takes out a sports jacket and trousers.
MONTY: You look a bit young.

MICK : Well, you need a young man for a job like this.
   MICK opens the wardrobe.
MONTY : Possibly. . . . Did you ever meet your predecessor?
MICK : Oswald?
MONTY : Oswald.
MICK : No . . . I've only been with the firm five weeks.
   MICK fishes a tonic bottle out of the bottom of the wardrobe;
   it is half full. He drinks from it and makes a face.
MONTY : That stuff's no good. I told him.
MICK : Why did he scarper?
MONTY : Luck. Opportunity. He took off.
MICK (cocky) : No stamina.
   MICK throws down the bottle.
MICK : That's what you've got to have in a job like this. Stamina.
You've got to have it. Providing, of course, you've got the technical
knowhow.
   He finds a litter of sexy magazines at the bottom of OSWALD'S
   wardrobe. He flicks through one, turning it to inspect the pose
   better.
MONTY : Nothing else?

MICK: What?
MONTY: Nothing else you need?
MICK: Well, you've got to have ambition.

    MICK tosses the magazine back in the bottom of the wardrobe.
    MARY calls softly from downstairs.

MARY (off-screen): Mr Travis?
MICK: Yes, Mrs Ball?
MARY (off-screen): I've got your supper ready. It's in the parlour.
MICK: Thank you, Mrs Ball. Be right down.

    As MONTY leaves:

MONTY: Watch out for her treacle tart. There's many a fly got stuck in that.

    BLACKOUT

    The following sequence intercuts between MICK practising his sales technique for the next day and ALAN and his group in the limbo setting, singing and playing the song, *Sell, Sell, Sell*.
    MICK is sitting on the chair in his bedroom. On the bed he has spread out the map of his territory, together with his customer call cards. (Small cards on which are typed details of the

customer's family, hobbies, etc.) He is marking a town on the map.

ALAN: *Sell . . . sell . . . sell . . . sell*
Everything you stand for
Tell . . . tell . . . tell . . . tell
All the people that you care for

MICK memorises a card.

ALAN: *Running here, running there,*
Keep it moving sonny, don't despair—
Because the next one will be, the next one will be,
The next one will be the best one of the year.

MICK practises (twice) his entrance to greet a customer.

ALAN: *Give . . . give . . . give . . . give*
Everything you're paid for
Run . . . run . . . run . . . run
For everything you've prayed for
Keep that smile . . .

MICK crosses to the wash basin to practise his sincere smile into the mirror. The camera zooms in closer as he takes his cheeks in his hands and forces a smile.

ALAN: *... on your face*
   With a smile you're welcome any place—
   Because the next one will be, the next one will be,
   MICK is in front of the mirror, a grotesque smile stuck on his face.
ALAN: *The next one will be the best one of the year ...*

ON THE ROAD
   Coal tips and pit buildings on the flat West Riding landscape. MICK's car drives along the road. The song continues ...
ALAN: *Can I interest you in this article of mine?*
   Can I interest you to spare some of your time?
   A small mining town. Travelling shot over the bonnet of MICK's car of the street ahead. He draws up outside a shop and prances inside.
ALAN: *Can I interest you in this life of mine?*
   Won't you listen, listen, listen, listen, listen ...
   Later. MICK is driving through another town.
   A huge empty canteen. MICK presents a packet of coffee to a bemused charlady.

Still driving, MICK pours Maltesers from a bag into his mouth. The street ahead over the bonnet of the travelling car. As MICK drives, he sorts out his calling cards.

ALAN : *Can I interest you in this article of mine?*
Can I interest you to spare some of your time?
Can I interest you in this life of mine?
Won't you listen, listen, listen, listen, listen . . .

MICK lifts two heavy cartons of coffee packets from the back of his car and staggers backwards into the village shop and up to the counter. We observe the scene through the store window. The homely lady shopkeeper smiles encouragingly as he puts the cartons down on the counter. He dips into them and takes some packets from each. Then he suggests that she takes more. The lady laughs pleasantly at the daring suggestion, but shakes her head.

ALAN : *Won't you sell, sell, sell—sell everything you stand for?*
Tell, tell, tell—tell all the people that you care for
Running here, running there
Keep it moving sonny, don't despair—
Because the next one will be, the next one will be,
The next one will be the best one of the year . . .

MICK is now back in his car, sorting out his calling cards again.

A LARGE STEEL WORKS

MICK drives up to the gate of the works, and stops. A notice stands beside the gate : 'AMALGAMATED STEEL & IRON WORKS COMMERCIAL VEHICLES ONLY ALL VEHICLES CHECK ON ENTRY.'

MICK goes over to the gatehouse, raps on the window and the black gateman looks up dourly and signals over his shoulder.

MICK goes to the gate and swings it open.

MICK's car drives through the complicated network of yards and roadways. The vast complex seems remarkably quiet. The car stops. MICK gets out and makes for a big shed-like building. The huge canteen, with its long tables and its self-service counter at the end, is empty. MICK calls out.

MICK : Good morning ! . . . Good morning !

An elderly CLEANER emerges.

MICK : Mrs Williams?
CLEANER : Who?
MICK : Mrs Williams. Catering Manageress.

CLEANER: She doesn't come in any more.
MICK: It's urgent.
CLEANER: There's nothing urgent around here. They're closing us down.
MICK: Closing you down?
CLEANER: Laying us off.
MICK: What? 5,000 men?
CLEANER: That's right. Redundant.
   She sits heavily.
   BLACKOUT

WAKEDALE ROAD
A main road. Cars drive by. MICK disconsolately sits in his car adding up the meagre total of his day's sales.
Insert of sales that day. The total sum reads: £5.97. He has not done well.
Suddenly MICK notices a large sign by the side of the road. Zoom into sign which reads: 'WELCOME TO WAKEDALE AND THE WAKEDALE HOTEL YORKSHIRE'S FINEST SWIMMING POOL HAUTE CUISINE.'

WAKEDALE HOTEL
Camera tilts down the façade of the impressive pile. Genteel music is playing.

WAKEDALE HOTEL FOYER
MICK moves up to the reception desk. The young LADY RECEPTIONIST, a self-possessed girl in a neat black dress, ostentatiously finishes what she is doing, then looks up.
MICK: Good evening. I'd like to see the catering manager—Mr Faulkner.
RECEPTIONIST: And . . . it's Mr—?
MICK: Travis. Imperial Coffee.
RECEPTIONIST: I'll see if he's still on duty . . . (She turns away, then looks back): You can sit down.
She lifts up an internal phone and dials. MICK crosses the lobby and takes a chair with his briefcase on his knees. He slides his call card out of his inside pocket and checks it discreetly. He practises his smile. A small, dapper man in a dark suit approaches, clearing his throat. MICK rises with plenty of spring and extends his hand.
MICK: Lovely evening, Mr Faulkner.
MANAGER: Charlie Johnson. Sit down lad . . . Panatella?
He offers MICK a cigar and sits beside him. He lights MICK's cigar.
MICK: Oh, thank you very much . . . thank you. Is Mr Faulkner off?
MANAGER: No, no. . . . But I'm the manager here. I like to keep my contacts personal.
MICK: Oh, so do I . . .
MANAGER: You'll be replacing your previous colleague?
MICK: Correct.
MANAGER: Mm . . . Sad business that . . . Still (conspiratorially): I take it the arrangements will be as were?
MICK (lost for a moment): Er—yes, Mr Johnson . . . yes.
MANAGER: It's Mayor Johnson to be precise. I've still got three months in office.
MICK: Oh!
MANAGER: Good—well, I'll give you all the help I can. Not only here but in Leeds, Doncaster, Wakefield and other cities of major importance surrounding. . . . You can confirm with Faulkner that we'll be continuing our standing bulk order—in fact you'll find him

round the back now. You've just come at the right time. We're having a bit of a party. Do you like you-know-what?

    He winks at MICK...

MICK: What, Mayor Johnson?
MANAGER: A party.
MICK: Oh yes! Absolutely delighted.
MANAGER: Right, come on then.

    The MANAGER rises and makes briskly for the back premises, raising the flap of the RECEPTIONIST's desk and passing through. MICK follows.

RECEPTIONIST: Good evening, Mayor.
MANAGER: Good evening. Have they fixed that TV set in the Rockingham Suite yet?
RECEPTIONIST: They're doing it now.
MANAGER: Good. (to MICK): Tele-Rent. Marvellous firm. I'm on the Board, you know. If ever you want a telly...
    BLACKOUT

HOTEL BACKYARD

    The MANAGER and MICK emerge into the night air and step

briskly past the kitchen wastebins.
MANAGER: Very fortunate—your coming on a Tuesday. . . . We always have a gathering on Tuesdays. You'll make some useful contacts. Always best to meet people when they're relaxed. Plenty of variety—promise you that.

They come up to a large shed-like structure. It is shuttered. A low light is shining above the door. The MANAGER knocks four times, deliberately.

NIGHTSPOT CLOAKROOM
A GIRL, sweet and well-upholstered, runs to the door, peeks through a spy-hole, then opens it to admit MICK and the MANAGER. She is dressed, like all the nightspot waitresses, in a tiny decorative apron that shows more than it hides.
LINDA: Good evening, Mr Mayor.
MANAGER: Linda. This is Mr Travis, Linda. That's Linda.
LINDA: Happy to greet you.
MICK (shaking hands): Pleased to meet you, too.
MANAGER: Got my coat, love. (to MICK): You'll enjoy yourself here, I can tell you . . .

LINDA takes MICK's briefcase, then helps the MANAGER, who removes the jacket of his suit, into a maroon velvet smoking jacket.

MANAGER (to LINDA): Ta!

MICK peers over the MANAGER's shoulder. They move on into the crowded darkness.

NIGHTSPOT

The MANAGER and MICK press through bystanders at the door of the dark shed. The place is packed. Men and girls sitting at little tables, an illuminated bar at the back, white-coated waiters and aproned girls flitting about. Decorations are garish and tatty.

The sound of a 16mm projector: this is standing on the bar, projecting a black-and-white picture onto a screen at the far end of the room. On the screen a plump, archly provocative Blonde is sitting on a bed in black bra and panties, removing her black stockings. She strokes her thigh sensually.

Appreciative chuckles from the audience. The MANAGER chuckles and leads MICK towards a table. As they cross the projector beam, their shadows interrupt the picture. The Blonde is removing her bra. Angry shouts. A man at the bar grabs MICK by the shoulder and pushes him out of the way.

The MANAGER leads MICK to a table where two men and three girls are already sitting round glasses and a whisky bottle. A girl climbs on a man's knee to make room for MICK.

The Blonde on the screen is now dressed in a skimpy black negligee. She runs to the fireplace, bends low and looks up the chimney. There is a Christmas tree in the corner of the room. She scampers back to bed.

MICK sits down and looks around. Everyone is glued to the screen.

A bulky Santa emerges from the fireplace. The Blonde snuggles excitedly into her pillow. Santa tiptoes to the end of the bed. The Blonde sits up in delicious alarm. Santa ogles, amazed. The camera zooms in. . . .

Cheers and laughter from a table of rugby players.

MICK watches with enjoyment.

Now sitting on the bed beside Santa, the Blonde sneaks her hand under his cloak, groping him. Santa throws her back on the bed and whisks her panties off. He unbuckles his belt and

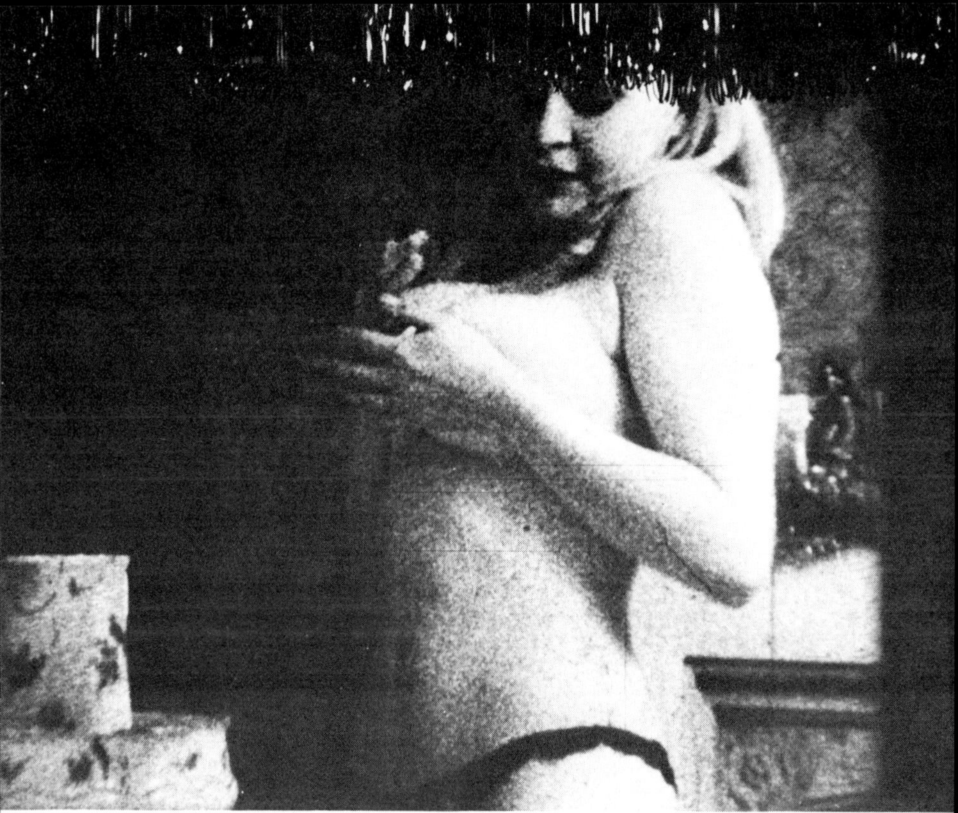

throws his cloak open. The audience cheers and applauds. The film ends and the lights come up. The COMPERE walks onto the stage and rolls the screen up. He applauds; the audience relaxes; waitresses bustle.

MICK looks around. A BUSINESS MAN pushes his way to their table. The MAYOR looks up.

BUSINESS MAN (WILSON): Hello, Mr Johnson.
MANAGER: Sit down, lad.
WILSON (nodding at MICK): New member.
MANAGER: Yes—this is Mr Travis of Imperial Coffee.
WILSON (grinning): Glad you could make it tonight. Harry Wilson—Tax Office.
MICK (reaching across to shake hands): Great pleasure to meet you.
MANAGER: Chief Inspector.
WILSON: Any little business problems you run up against—let me know.
MICK: Thank you very much.

From the other side of the table a sporty type in a bow tie reaches across—

NEWSPAPER EDITOR: Attenborough. (Shaking hands): I edit the local rag.
MICK: Oh—very pleased to meet you.
NEWSPAPER EDITOR: And this is Jackie.
JACKIE (a long-legged redhead): Happy to greet you.
MICK: A pleasure.
MANAGER (proprietorially): *Wakedale Echo*. Invaluable to a man in your line. Comes out every Thursday. (He gestures across the table): Have you met Maureen? Maureen—say hello to Mr Travis.
MICK: Oh—how do you do?

The man on MICK's right introduces himself.

POLICE SUPERINTENDENT: Pleased to meet you, Mr Travis. Barlow. County Constabulary.
MICK: Pleased to meet you.
MANAGER: Superintendent.
POLICE SUPERINTENDENT: At your service . . . (Introducing his girl, who is sitting on his knee): Oh, this is Mavis. Now you be nice to Mr Travis, Mavis. But not too nice. (He roars with laughter.)
MAVIS (shaking hands): Happy to greet you.
MICK: Great pleasure.
POLICE SUPERINTENDENT (cuddling MAVIS): Come here . . .

On the stage the COMPERE steps forward to a roll of drums and

makes an announcement into the microphone.

COMPERE: And now, Ladies and Gentlemen, we come to the part of the show you've all been waiting for (Cheers . . . The COMPERE leers): We have a first-class selection for you tonight—all your favourites—and one or two novelties. And as usual, we'll be starting with our request spot—so if you'd like to signify your preference in the usual manner . . .

COMPERE pauses, waiting for requests.

WILSON: Isle of Capri.

Laughter and cheers.

MANAGER: Well done, Harry.

POLICE SUPERINTENDENT: Tutti Frutti.

OTHERS: Whiplash!! Isle of Capri!!

FOOTBALLER: Roman Candles.

COMPERE: Roman Candles—Another one?

VOICE FROM THE BACK: Chocolate Sandwich!

MANAGER: Yes—Chocolate Sandwich!

MICK takes a drink and looks around as the cry for 'Chocolate Sandwich' is taken up.

The table of Rugby footballers turn it into a chant.

GENERAL SHOUT: Cho—clate Sand—wich! Cho—clate Sand—wich!

The MANAGER joins in, clapping the beat.

MICK, smoking and drinking, shouts too.

MICK: Cho—clate Sand—wich!

The COMPERE holds up his hands for silence. He shouts through the noise.

COMPERE: All right—all right— all right! All right, Ladies and Gentlemen. You have it—you have it! Ladies and Gentlemen, by overwhelming demand we start with everybody's favourite—Chocolate Sandwich! All right, June—Violet—Eddie. Come on, loves.

The COMPERE gestures down into the audience, then withdraws to the side of the stage. Two girls and a West Indian climb up on the stage. The audience cheers and laughs as they let down a large folding bed from the back of the stage. A heavy vamp from the band. The girls start to strip.

As MICK drinks, watching—a pert girl, REBECCA, takes his glass from him and drinks.

MICK (with drunken formality): Travis—Imperial Coffee.

REBECCA: Beckie. Mind if I borrow your knee? (MICK slaps his knee invitingly): Thank you—good evening. (She sits on his knee.)

The whole party is watching the stage attentively. JUNE and VIOLET are now naked, rhythmically dancing to the music, with EDDIE in the centre. In the audience a large business man seated between two giggling girls begins to strip in time to the music. JACKIE, the NEWSPAPER EDITOR's girlfriend, sensuously bites his thumb. MICK watches greedily as the Chocolate Sandwich nears its climax. REBECCA pours whisky alternately down his throat and hers. The music grows louder. MICK grins lecherously.
BLACKOUT

SUTHERLAND HOUSE DRIVEWAY
MICK's car brakes to a halt in the drive. He gets out, remembers something and reaches back into the car. He lifts a case of whisky off the front seat and staggers with it into the house.

SUTHERLAND HOUSE HALL
MICK falls back against the front door, slamming it shut.

MICK'S ROOM
MICK pushes the door open with his foot. He switches on the light with his free hand, closes the door with his body, and crosses the room, putting the box down by the chest of drawers. He slips off his coat and staggers to the washbasin. As he passes the mirror on the chest of drawers we see the reflection of his bed. MARY BALL is lying in it. She switches on the bedside light. MICK looks up into the mirror above the basin.
MARY: Michael...
MICK (turning, pleasantly stupefied): Mrs Ball...
MARY holds out her arms towards him. She seems to be naked.
MARY: Mary.
MICK totters towards the bed, towel in hand. He drops his towel down on the bed as MARY's arms grip him tightly. They embrace. He kicks off a shoe. BLACKOUT: the other shoe drops. Pause. The telephone rings.

SUTHERLAND HOUSE HALL
Everything is still. The telephone is ringing.

MICK'S ROOM
MARY is sleeping in MICK's arms. His eyes open. Footsteps are

heard coming up the stairs.
The door opens and the light is switched on. BILL is at the door. He looks at the bed, expressionless.
BILL: Mr Travis. Wanted on phone. Urgent.
He leaves.
MICK eases himself out of MARY's clutches, slips out of bed and pulls on his trousers and braces.

SUTHERLAND HOUSE HALL
MICK runs down the stairs and picks up the phone. BILL appears and stands at the bottom of the stairs, listening.
MICK: Hello?... Hello... Gloria! What? What's that...? (He listens): Scotland! As well?!... (Camera closes in on him): I haven't any warm clothing... Yes. But I'm doing well here—building up some fabulous contacts—I don't want to throw it away... Yes, I see it's a challenge... Tomorrow?... But where?... That's two hundred miles away... By 10 a.m.... Who do I ask for?... Who?... Who?... Hello... Hello... Gloria, hello....
The line is cut off. The phone goes dead. MICK taps the receiver. He hangs up. BILL watches him as he walks past him on his way upstairs.

LANDING
MICK walks up the stairs. On the landing he pauses. MARY is standing in his doorway. There is the sound of a voice.
MONTY: Mr Travis!
MICK looks and sees MONTY standing at his door. He holds up his hand and beckons MICK. MICK hesitates, then walks along to MONTY's room.

MONTY'S ROOM
As MICK enters the room, MONTY walks towards the wardrobe. We see MONTY's tailoring equipment—a sewing machine, an ironing board.
MICK: Did you hear that? Do you think I ought to go?
MONTY: I've got something for you.
On a tailor's dummy at the end of the room there is a gold jacket with black velvet collar and cuffs. MONTY slowly spins the dummy round for MICK to see.
A magical arpeggio of music.
MONTY: Come on, try it on. Arms up.

Mick moves towards him and puts on the gold jacket.
Monty: A perfect fit!
Monty helps him with it, smoothing it and pulling down the back. Mick admires the fit and the gleaming material.
Mick: It's good. It really is good.
Monty hands him the trousers with a black polythene bag.
Monty: You'll find it surprisingly warm.
Another magical chord. Mick stands a moment, looking at Monty.

MICK'S ROOM
Mick has dressed now and is ready to leave. He holds his suitcase in one hand and the black plastic bag containing the gold suit in the other. Mary hangs his binoculars around his neck, with a sad smile.
Mick: I'll be back. I promise I will.
Mary tries to smile back: but she knows . . . Mick kisses her goodbye and leaves the room.

Mick hurries down the passage and down the stairs. Monty

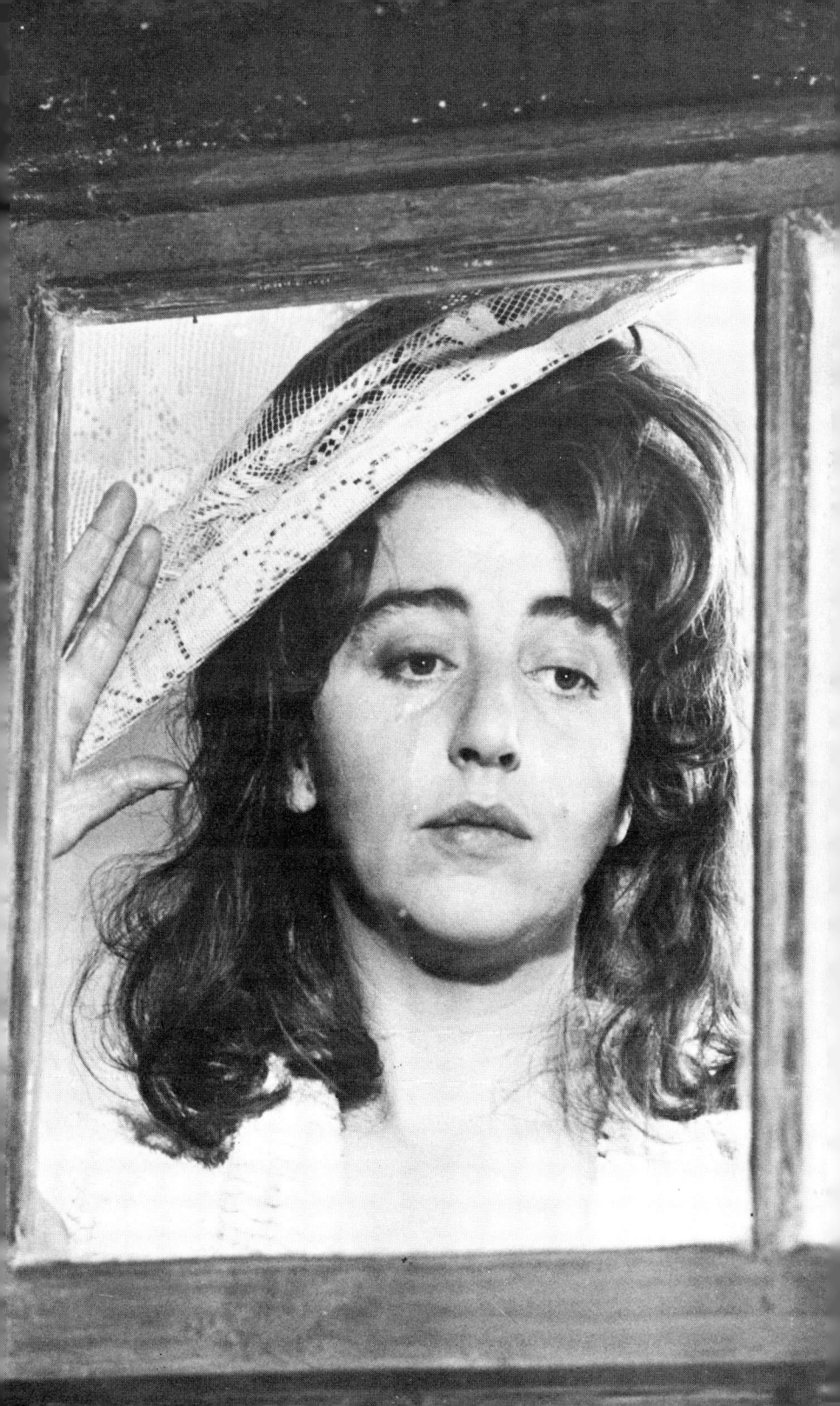

emerges to stand by the bannister. He calls after him.
MONTY: Try not to die like a dog.
MICK turns back, surprised. BILL has climbed up the stairs towards him and taken the suitcase from his hand. MONTY retreats. MICK turns and follows BILL down the stairs.

SUTHERLAND HOUSE DRIVEWAY
BILL follows MICK down the steps. He carries MICK's case to the back of his car.

BEDROOM WINDOW
MARY comes to the window. Drawing the lace curtains gently aside, she looks down into the driveway. Camera moves in closer. Tears fill her eyes.

DRIVEWAY
From MARY's point of view we see MICK about to get into the car. BILL hovers. MICK gives him a tip. Before MICK gets into the car he gives a last look up to MARY at the window.

BEDROOM WINDOW
Tears stream down MARY's face.

DRIVEWAY
MICK closes the car door and drives away as MARY watches sadly from the window.
BLACKOUT

TITLE: *NORTH*

NORTHUMBERLAND LANDSCAPE MICK'S CAR
MICK's car is driving along a lonely road across bare, featureless, heath-covered hill country. The end of the hymn, *O Jesus I have promised,* is heard on the radio.
MICK, whistling, adjusts the tuning on his radio. The programme continues with a prayer.
RADIO VOICE: *'The Blessing'.*
> *Lord, on the way to Goodness,*
> *When we stumble, hold us—*
> *When we fall, lift us up.*
> *When we are hard-pressed by Evil, deliver us.*

At this moment, MICK props his map up in front of him.
BLACKOUT

NORTHUMBERLAND ROAD
The camera pans from six sheep crossing the road to MICK's car, now stationary at the side of the empty road. MICK is standing next to the car. He is shaving with an electric shaver, reading his map at the same time. He puts away his shaver and continues studying his map. He looks across the open landscape.

RADIO VOICE: . . . *at last. After Soyuz II braking system for re-entry into the earth's atmosphere was switched off—a soft-landing engine fired according to plan and a smooth landing was made in the arranged area, presumably somewhere in Khazakstan. A helicopter-borne recovering crew which landed simultaneously with Soyuz II opened the hatch and found the three cosmonauts dead.*
BLACKOUT

NORTHUMBERLAND LANDSCAPE
MICK's car turns off the main road to plunge down a steep hill.

The radio plays a few bars of Japanese religious music, which fades into an interview.

QUESTION: *Now, Za Zen, what does that mean?*

ANSWER: *Za Zen is a way of sitting cross-legged and with an erect back, practising the art of Zen...*

Inside MICK's car the transistor set swings in front of his head as he drives past a sign on the side of the road which reads: 'GOVERNMENT PROPERTY NO ENTRY WITHOUT PERMISSION'.

QUESTION: *And Zen means?*

ANSWER: *To understand life, to be with life, to ... get a feeling of life ... So that in effect all your days are good days; and every day should be looked upon as living in the moment ...*

MICK draws up at some barbed wire fencing. Another notice. He gets out and looks around...

ANSWER: *... rather than in the past or in the future—and this is really what Zen is all about—living now.*

MICK stands consulting his map. He reaches into the car to bring out a pair of binoculars, and climbs up onto the roof of the car. Standing on the car, he sweeps the horizon with his binoculars.

QUESTION: *Now tell me how we come by this illumination—this awareness that is at the heart of the practice called Za Zen?*

Through the binoculars we see first the empty landscape, then alight on three huge white metal globes.

ANSWER: *It is very hard practice. Nothing is acquired in a day.*

QUESTION: *And yet I understand that this illumination does come suddenly ...*

At this moment the sound of two motor vehicles is heard. MICK looks round in surprise as soldiers in an Army truck and scout car drive up alongside MICK's car.

ANSWER: *It comes suddenly. It comes in many ways. One could be arranging a vase of flowers ... one could be sitting cross-legged with a straight back ... one could be doing so many things ...*

A CAPTAIN in a beret and khaki wool sweater leans out of the scout car and calls up to MICK.

CAPTAIN: I'm asking you not to give any trouble. I want you on the ground before I count three ... One ... Two ...

MICK: Christ—I'm only trying to find out where I am.

MICK slithers to the ground. Three armed soldiers come forward from the truck and pinion his arms on both sides.

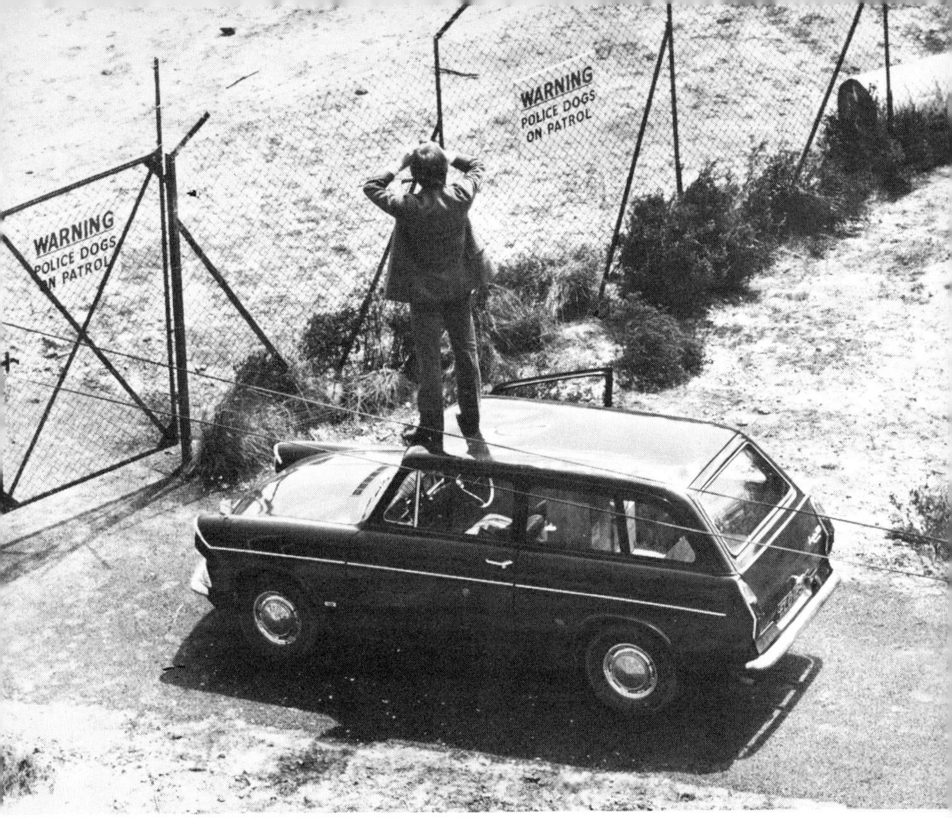
WARNING
POLICE DOGS
ON PATROL
WARNING
POLICE DOGS
ON PATROL

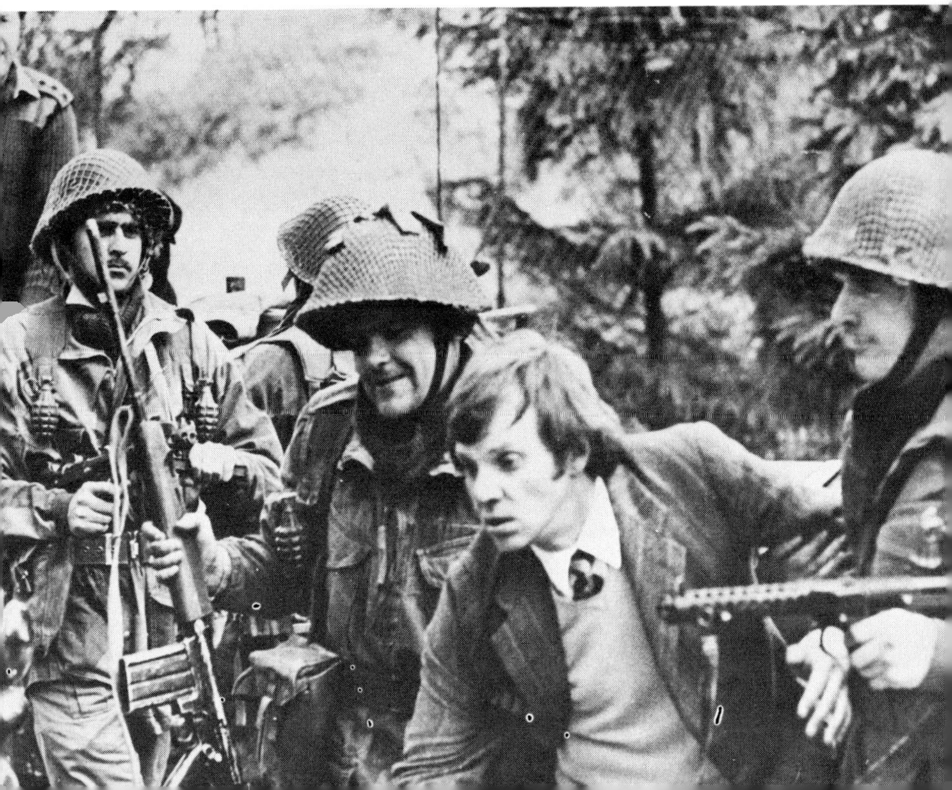

CAPTAIN: Don't kick, don't butt with your head—and you won't get hurt. OK chaps, get him in.
    They drag him into the back of the truck. A black bag goes over his head. The vehicles drive off. MICK's car is left, the radio still playing.
RADIO VOICE: . . . *there will be rain and drizzle at times* . . .

ATOMIC RESEARCH ESTABLISHMENT
The scout car, followed by the truck, drives along by an electrified fence. It turns in at an entrance closed by a counter-weighted barrier. A guard salutes and raises the barrier.
The cortege drives across a wide concrete area. They pass two scientists in white coats, and disappear into a square, concrete aperture.
Two guards in police-force navy blue and peaked caps, lead MICK down a bare, windowless passage. The atmosphere is heavy with a pervasive electronic hum.
A door opens into a dark room. The light clicks on. MICK is shoved down into a chair. The black bag is removed. The guards leave him.
The room has no windows. A small table, two chairs and a hat stand. There is a picture of the Queen on the wall, and on another wall is a large poster-type picture of an English Landscape. There is another door in the corner opposite the door of MICK's entry. MICK sits for a moment in silence. He gets up and tries the door. It is locked. He strolls round the room and decides to try the second door. It opens.
MICK finds himself in another corridor. The hum deepens, grows more intense. He makes his way cautiously down it, and comes to a staircase at the end. A sign on the wall reads: 'PERSONNEL FORBIDDEN BEYOND THIS POINT'. MICK goes up.
MICK finds himself in some kind of control room, all steel and dials. He looks around and taps a dial. Then he moves to an observation window. Looking down through glass pannelling he sees two men wearing protective space suits. Their movements are strange and slow, as if through the haze of vapourized gases. They are lifting some object into the mouth of a glowing machine.
As MICK watches an arm suddenly comes round his neck, pinioning him. He struggles but is held firm. He is led away.

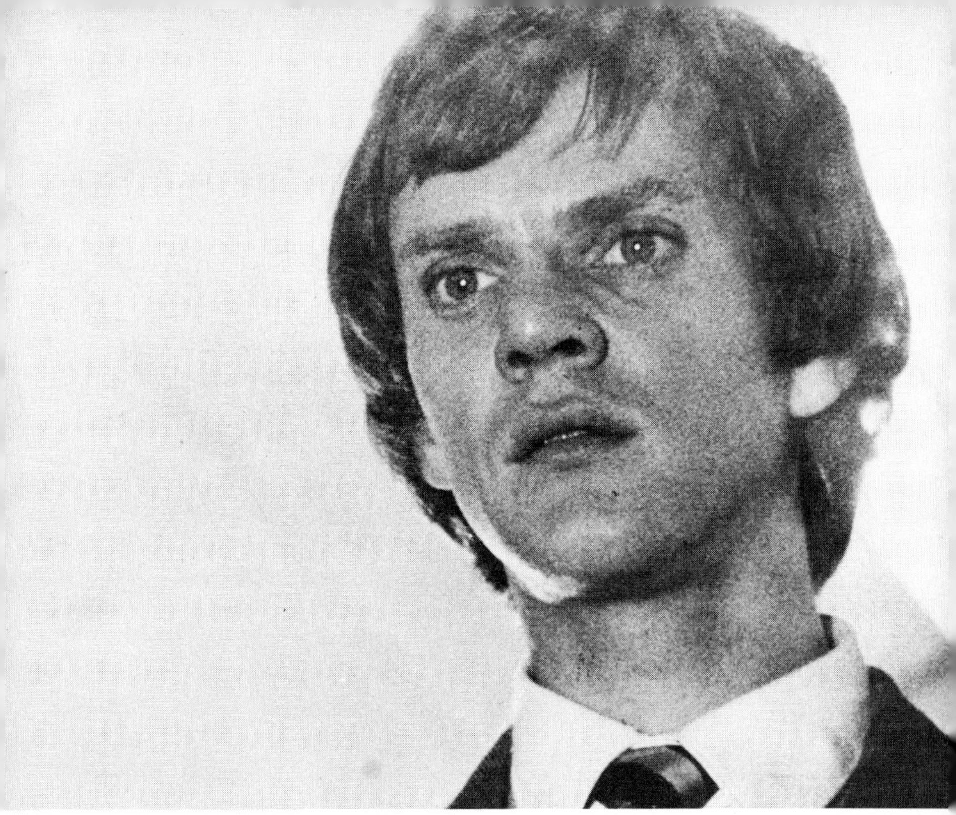

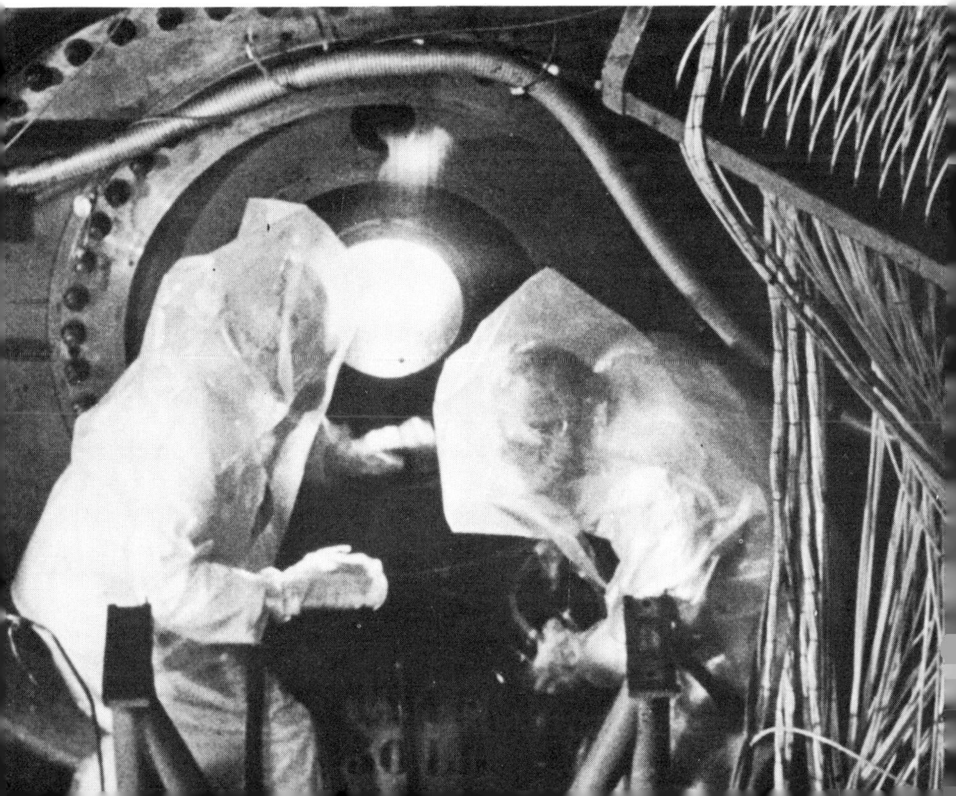

INTERROGATION ROOM
Another bare windowless room. An old desk (over it another picture of the Queen) with an old-fashioned telephone on it. A simple hanging lamp with a domestic-type shade. An old chair with arms and a high back, in which MICK will be seated, and two other chairs.
A GUARD leads MICK beneath the lamp, sits him down and undoes the blindfold over his eyes. The GUARD falls back against the wall. Two INTERROGATORS are sitting in front of MICK at the desk, on straight-backed chairs. They have dossiers which they consult. MICK'S case of samples is lying on the desk. The INTERROGATORS are civilians, in suits. One is quite young; the other definitely senior—he has the air of a bank manager.
SENIOR INTERROGATOR: Now, Mr Travis. You realise where you are?
MICK is too dazed and confused to answer. The INTERROGATOR speaks again, smooth and measured.
SENIOR INTERROGATOR: You know where you are, Mr Travis.
MICK: Yes.
SENIOR INTERROGATOR: Your pass.
MICK'S hand goes up to his pocket. The GUARD takes a step, but the INTERROGATOR waves him back. MICK gives his salesman's card to the SENIOR INTERROGATOR, who glances at it and passes it to the JUNIOR INTERROGATOR.
SENIOR INTERROGATOR: What's in these packets?
He picks up a sample pack from the desk.
MICK: Coffee samples.
The JUNIOR INTERROGATOR takes the packet and slits it open. Beans pour out. MICK tries to be bold.
MICK: Hey—that happens to be Company property. I have to account for every single bean. Otherwise I'm in trouble.
The JUNIOR INTERROGATOR sniffs the beans.
JUNIOR INTERROGATOR: You are in trouble.
SENIOR INTERROGATOR: Who are you working for?
MICK: Gloria Rowe.
SENIOR INTERROGATOR: Who else?
MICK (cheeky): What do you mean 'who else'?
The JUNIOR INTERROGATOR leans forward and suddenly hits MICK viciously across the mouth.
SENIOR INTERROGATOR: Who are you working for?
MICK (tamed, his mouth beginning to bleed): The Imperial Coffee

Company.

SENIOR INTERROGATOR: Who do you know in this establishment?

MICK: I don't know anybody.

SENIOR INTERROGATOR (signs of impatience): But who were you expecting to contact?

A slight pause.

MICK: The catering manager. Mr Woolley. Has three children. Plays billiards.

The SENIOR INTERROGATOR glances at the JUNIOR INTERROGATOR, who consults a list of names in a folder. Meanwhile the SENIOR INTERROGATOR produces a document which he hands to MICK. He holds out a pen.

SENIOR INTERROGATOR: Sign this, please. Where the crosses are.

MICK: What is it?

SENIOR INTERROGATOR: Your confession.

MICK: But I don't know what I've done. I haven't done anything.

The SENIOR INTERROGATOR glances at the JUNIOR, who has consulted his lists. He shakes his head negatively. The SENIOR INTERROGATOR turns back to MICK.

SENIOR INTERROGATOR: You'll find it easier if you sign.

MICK (loudly): I haven't done anything.

SENIOR INTERROGATOR: Basset!

The SENIOR INTERROGATOR nods to the GUARD, who steps forward to strap MICK'S wrists to the chair. As he straps them, MICK tries to undo them. MICK struggles as BASSET puts a thick strap round his neck which holds him rigid. During this operation there is a knock on the door, which is pushed open by an elderly TEA-LADY, a homely body who pulls her tea trolley, complete with urn, cups, teapot, sugar basin, teaspoons and plate of biscuits. She is wearing a pink nylon overall and pink tea-lady's hat.

TEA-LADY: Tea or coffee?

SENIOR INTERROGATOR: Tea please. Two sugars.

JUNIOR INTERROGATOR: Er—coffee—black.... Thank you.

SENIOR INTERROGATOR: Tea, Basset?

GUARD (a nice smile): No thank you, sir.

TEA-LADY: Chocolate biscuit?

SENIOR INTERROGATOR: Please.

The SENIOR INTERROGATOR nods assent, and the TEA-LADY hands him one on a plate.

TEA-LADY: That'll be 3p for the biscuit. Would the young man like

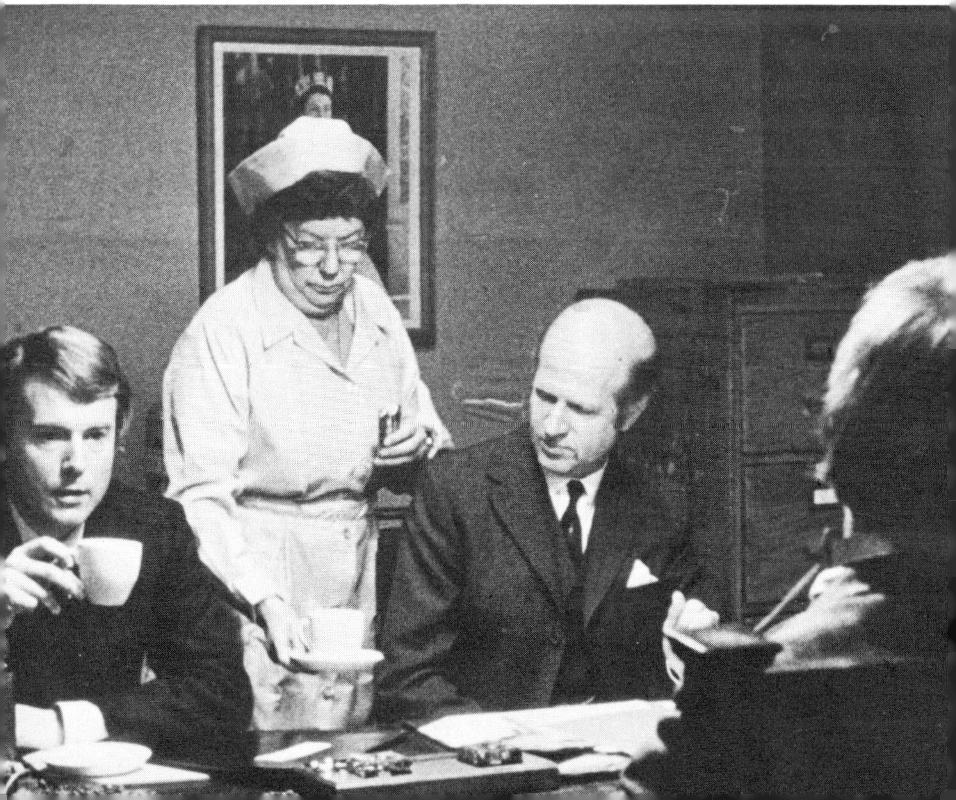

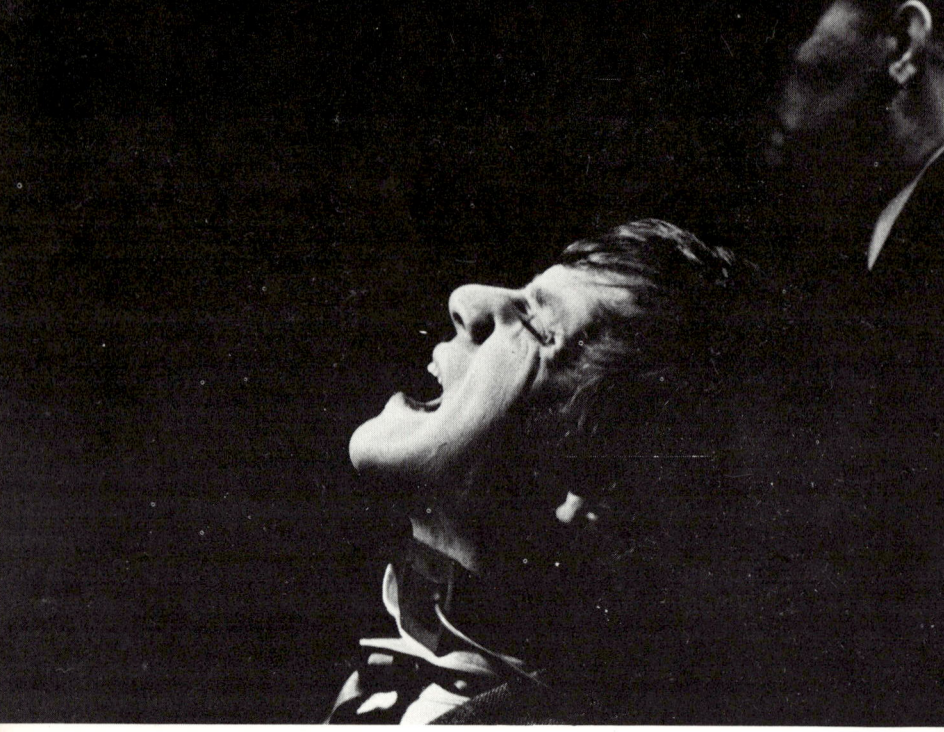

a cup of tea?

SENIOR INTERROGATOR (paying her): Later.

The TEA-LADY clucks sympathetically and manoeuvres herself and her trolley out of the room.

SENIOR INTERROGATOR (stirring his tea): Now there's no need to go through all this you know! You've only got to sign the paper.

MICK (frightened now): But I'm innocent. I haven't done anything.

The SENIOR INTERROGATOR gives a nod to the JUNIOR, who turns the generator handle—quite gently. MICK tenses and whimpers. The SENIOR INTERROGATOR leans forward.

SENIOR INTERROGATOR: In der Sondheit oder die Fahrenheit betrogen wir uber die grenze?

MICK looks blankly at him. A sharper turn on the generator handle. He cries out.

SENIOR INTERROGATOR: Chesh stakan chaiu boriego phunt sacharu?

MICK cries again, in agony.

SENIOR INTERROGATOR: There are three things you can be sure of: the pain is not going to stop—you will remain conscious—and in the end you will sign. . . .

The JUNIOR INTERROGATOR gives the handle a savage and sustained twist. MICK screams. The SENIOR INTERROGATOR looks to the GUARD, who steps forward and unties the straps around MICK's right arm and neck. As he does this there is the sound of an alarm hooter from the recesses of the building. The JUNIOR INTERROGATOR rises and leaves the room. The SENIOR INTERROGATOR passes the confession to MICK and holds out the pen for him. MICK signs painfully. He passes the document back to the SENIOR INTERROGATOR, who reaches for the pen. As he takes it, the GUARD again ties down MICK's arm. The JUNIOR INTERROGATOR returns, murmurs something in the SENIOR INTERROGATOR's ear, and sits down again.

SENIOR INTERROGATOR : Now let's start at the beginning. When did you join the party?
MICK : Last year.
SENIOR INTERROGATOR : How much are they paying you?
MICK : Three hundred a month.
JUNIOR INTERROGATOR : Three hundred what . . . . ?
MICK : Pounds. . . (The INTERROGATOR looks at him) . . . Roubles.
SENIOR INTERROGATOR : Was your Headmaster correct to expel you from school?
MICK : Yes.
SENIOR INTERROGATOR : Do you believe that children are the hope of the future?
MICK : Yes.
SENIOR INTERROGATOR : Do you believe in the fellowship of men?
MICK : Yes.
JUNIOR INTERROGATOR : Think carefully.
MICK : . . . No.
SENIOR INTERROGATOR : Do you rate loyalty above obedience?

As MICK is hesitating over the answer the alarm sounds again, this time much louder and more insistent. The INTERROGATORS rise, collecting their documents. Together they leave the room. For a long moment MICK is left sitting, still fastened in his chair, with the GUARD impassively standing by. The alarms break off : footsteps hurry past outside and vanish into silence. The GUARD begins to worry; suddenly he breaks away and runs out of the door.
Another long moment. The GUARD has left the door open. Footsteps approach, then the TEA-LADY comes past the open door, tray in hand, methodically carrying on with her work. She sighs as she sees the discarded cups and plates, and MICK.

TEA-LADY : Always leave everything in a mess. I keep telling them.
She looks at MICK and 'tuts'. She undoes MICK's wrists. As she
collects the cups, he frees himself. He stands very groggily, then
runs from the room.
The TEA-LADY goes on cleaning coffee-beans off the table.

OUTSIDE
Everything is confusion : the alarms are going full blast, people
running, whistles blowing, Army trucks driving noisily past.
MICK slips out of a back door in the building, rubbing his sore
neck.
MICK looks around horrified. Thick black smoke is pouring
from one of the buildings. Men in white coats, panic stricken,
come running down the ramp. A menacing roar.
The gate and entrance. Chaos reigns. Motorcycles, ambulances, fire engines and Army trucks drive noisily in through
the gates. People are running in every direction. MICK runs to
the gate just avoiding a fire engine. Uniformed guards attempt
to direct the hysterical people out of the gate—and the traffic
in.

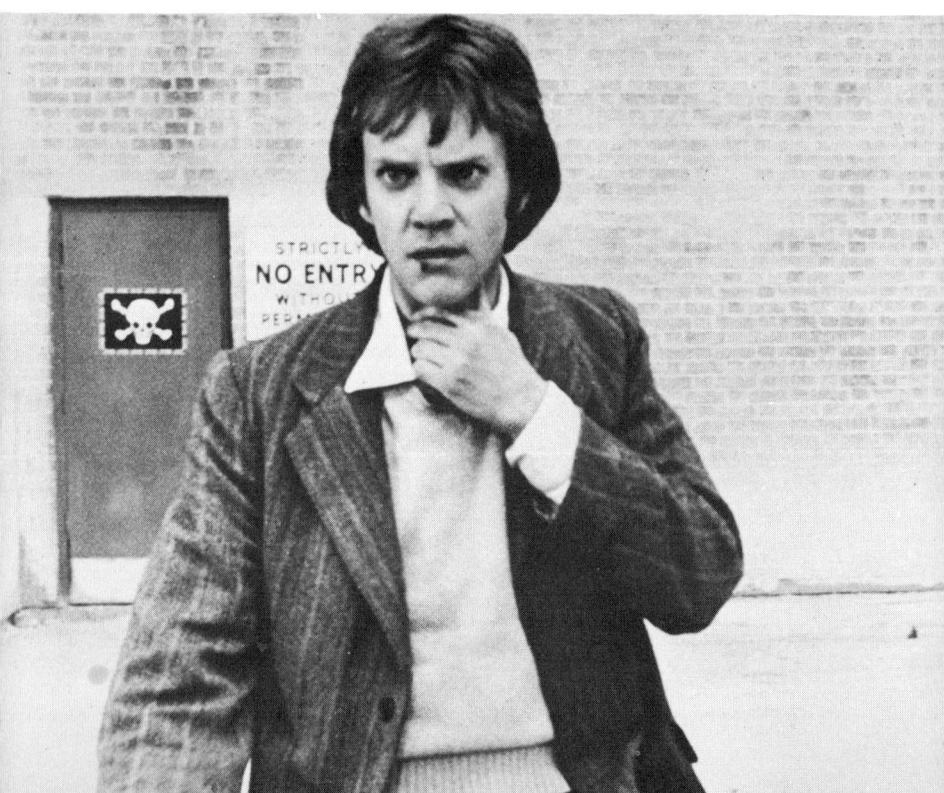

Mick makes his escape. He crosses the road and hurtles through the hedge on the other side.

The siren is still blowing. Mick runs desperately across a wide stretch of open country, the noise of alarm fading behind him. He starts up a hill. He is running faster now, looking behind him all the time. The blast of an explosion. Mick is blown off his feet. He gets up. Suddenly there is another immense explosion: a blinding flash lights up the sky. He is blown off his feet again.

In succession, a series of further explosions. Blinding flashes light up the sky. A huge column of smoke drifts up from behind Mick as he stumbles and falls on his way up the hill.

Mick reaches the top as burning debris falls out of the sky.

Mick runs through a wood; burnt, blackened trees surround him. He is looking everywhere for his car.

Suddenly he hears the sound of the radio; he sees his car below him, beginning to burn.

RADIO VOICE: *Headwell Secondary School in Jarrow, County Durham, recently began a project to clear the local dean; a piece of woodland.*

WOMAN'S VOICE: *The whole school, with the help of the Cleansing Department of the local authorities, cleared five wagon-loads of rubbish. Small parties deepened the channel of the stream, and did field study and sketching with a view to doing future landscape drawings. Others planted forty trees with the help of the Clerks Department. This is to be an annual affair, and this Spring we're building a footbridge...*

MICK slides down a long rugged slope. He runs to the car and opens the back door: smoke and fumes gush out at him as he tries to reach for his case. He is forced to retreat. He tries the side door and fights back the flames with his gold suit in the black plastic cover. He is trying to save his transistor radio now, but again he is forced to retreat. As MICK backs away the car blows up and bursts into flames. MICK is once again blown back off his feet. The gold suit is blown out of his hands...
MICK watches the car burn. . . . He looks around and sees his gold suit hanging on the wire fence. He goes to retrieve it.
A magical arpeggio of music.
As MICK has retrieved the suit a sudden deluge of water—either a sharp storm or some strange afterbirth from the atomic explosion—pours from the sky. A gale-like wind sweeps over the hill. MICK tries to shelter under the suit in its black plastic bag. Camera zooms into close-up of his desolate face.
The car is a black wreck—smoke still comes from it. Bizarre music starts to play.
BLACKOUT

SCORCHED EARTH
MICK, now wearing his gold suit, steps forward through the smoke and flames over scorched earth and burning trees. He staggers on through the smoke. After a while he hears the sound of water. He runs down a hill to find a stream between two banks of fresh earth. He falls down beside the stream, bathes his face and drinks from the cool, fresh water. Then he lies back on the grass. In the clean air, the peaceful summer sound of birds singing. In the distance a church bell begins to ring. MICK opens his eyes and sits up. He crosses the stream. The church bell is louder. MICK passes through a wood echoing with bird song, and comes to the top of a green hill. He looks down.

A SUNLIT VALLEY
MICK sees a country church from which the bell is sounding. People are streaming towards it over the rich green turf. Sheep are grazing. A horse-drawn farm cart carrying a church-going party moves towards the church. The bell stops. There is the sound of a hymn being sung. MICK moves forward from the hill.

CONGREGATION (singing off-screen): *Alleluia! Not as orphans*
Are we left in sorrow now;
Alleluia! He is near us,
Faith believes nor questions
how.

THE CHURCH
A lighted Norman window. MICK walks up the path between the gravestones to the church door. He enters.

MICK moves forward from the door to stand looking into the church through a wooden screen at the back. There is quite a large congregation, but the rear few rows of pews are empty. The people are rural, neat, respectable, healthy—the whole place is redolent of 'pure religion breathing household laws'. Altar, walls and window sills are decorated with flowers, fruits and vegetables, as if for harvest festival. MICK opens the door in the screen and steps forward. He stands at the top of the steps. The VICAR's WIFE, playing the organ beside the screen, does not see him. The congregation finish the hymn.

CONGREGATION (singing): *Though the cloud from sight removed him*
When the forty days were o'er,
Shall our hearts forget his promise,
'I am with you evermore'?

VICAR: Let us pray.
The congregation kneels. MICK moves unsteadily down the steps: suddenly weak, he sits in the rear pew.

VICAR: Almighty and most merciful Father—
The congregation echoes him.

CONGREGATION: Almighty and most merciful Father

VICAR: We thine unworthy servants—

CONGREGATION: We thine unworthy servants

VICAR: Do give thee most humble and hearty thanks—

CONGREGATION: Do give thee most humble and hearty thanks

VICAR: For all thy goodness and loving-kindness to us and to all men;

CONGREGATION : For all thy goodness and loving-kindness to us and to all men;
    MICK feels faint. His weakness overwhelms him. He keels over and vanishes from sight behind the oak pew.
    BLACKOUT

    The voices continue, fading into silence.
VICAR : We bless thee for our creation,
CONGREGATION : We bless thee for our creation,
VICAR : Preservation
CONGREGATION : Preservation

    THE VALLEY
    Morning.

    THE CHURCH
The VICAR'S WIFE with her three children—a girl of about nine, a little boy of seven, and a baby (18 months)—are working in the church, carrying out the fruit and flowers.
The VICAR'S WIFE is working near the pulpit. MICK wakes up

and looks over the edge of the pew. He sees the VICAR'S WIFE hand a sheaf of wheat to the little boy, a bunch of flowers to the girl. They carry them out into the sunshine. MICK watches as the VICAR'S WIFE picks up the small child and a basket and goes out through the chancel. He rises, pulling himself with an effort to his feet. He sees the harvest loaves surrounded with apples and tomatoes, and a profusion of flowers and vegetables at the base of the altar. Unsteadily he walks towards it. He sits on the altar steps and stretches out his hand for a loaf.

The VICAR'S WIFE enters and sees MICK. Her voice rings out.
VICAR'S WIFE: No, No! Not that! That's God's food. That's for God.

MICK looks round in alarm. The VICAR'S WIFE comes up to him.
VICAR'S WIFE: You're only a boy...

She kneels down by him and gathers him into her arms. MICK looks up, exhausted. She gives him her large full breast to suck. MICK drinks gratefully. She looks up, fulfilled.

The children play in the sunny churchyard outside. Thick

grasses and wild flowers grow among the old tombstones.
The VICAR'S WIFE holding her baby comes out on to the church porch followed by MICK. She points out, down the path.

VICAR'S WIFE (to MICK): Keep on there—go straight across the fields and through the woods. You'll find the motorway. Go South. Kit, May. (The children run up): Remember, go South. The children will show you the way. There's nothing in the North for a boy like you.

GIRL: Come on.

The two children run off.

MICK follows. He rests his hand on MAY's head. At the gate he turns and waves. The VICAR'S WIFE, standing in the porch holding her baby, raises her hand and waves back.

Pastoral music starts.

THE VALLEY

MAY and KIT run on ahead of MICK down the grassy slope of the valley. KIT leaps and jumps. MAY is holding a stem of blue flowers. MICK uses a small branch for a staff. They pass a huge,

spreading tree. The valley opens before them. MICK hands MAY his staff, puts the little boy on his shoulders and runs with him.

They reach a gate. MICK passes through; the children clamber up on the bars. MAY hands him back his staff and points the way.

MICK passes on along the track, beside a golden cornfield. He turns and waves to the children. Perched on the gate, at the doorway to the valley, the children wave back.

MICK turns and strides on his way.

The path takes him through an echoing wood. At the edge he stops a moment, then steps towards the sound of distant traffic.

THE MOTORWAY

MICK climbs a stile and runs down a grass slope towards a busy dual carriageway. He walks along signalling to hitch a lift from the passing cars. A large black saloon slows as it passes him, pulls in to the side and stops. As MICK runs up, the front passenger's door of the car opens and a MALE NURSE in a white coat looks out. A huge green road sign reads: 'THE

SOUTH—LONDON 250 MILES'.
MALE NURSE: Where are you making for?
MICK: London.
MALE NURSE (getting out): In a hurry?
MICK: Why?
MALE NURSE: Like to pick up some spare cash?
MICK: What for?
MALE NURSE: Nothing much. Scientific research. Medical. You know the kind of thing. We need volunteers.

    MICK glances into the car. He sees an OLD LADY sitting in the back. She smiles endearingly at him and gives a little wave.

MICK: How much?
MALE NURSE: A hundred quid.
MICK: A hundred and fifty, and you're on.
MALE NURSE: I'm not authorised to vary the terms, sir. But if you'd like to come up to the Centre you could talk it over with the Chief.

    The MALE NURSE opens the back door of the car. MICK steps up jauntily, throws his staff away and climbs in.

MICK: OK—OK—OK.

The limousine drives off.
BLACKOUT

COUNTRY ROAD
The car turns off the main road into a wooded drive. There is a lodge at the gate and a notice: 'MILLAR RESEARCH CLINIC—PRIVATE'.

THE MILLAR CLINIC
The car drives smoothly up to a palatial country house. Smooth lawns surround the house, which has a white columned portico and a central dome. The car stops and the MALE NURSE gets out.

MILLAR CLINIC HALL
The large hall, now the Reception Department for the Clinic, is busy. Nurses are carrying trays of medicine and X-rays. A male nurse is operating a switchboard. Notices give directions to Lecture Halls, Wards ('A', 'B', 'C', etc.), Operating Theatres and Experimental Wing. Two porters lounge beside a row of invalid chairs, reading the sports pages of the *Sun* and the *Daily Mirror*. A LADY REGISTRAR in a white uniform comes from behind a control desk to greet the arrivals.
LADY REGISTRAR: Good morning.
MICK: Morning.
LADY REGISTRAR: Welcome to the Millar Clinic. Will you take a chair, please.
The MALE NURSE guides the OLD LADY over to the row of wheel chairs as MICK has a look round. The LADY REGISTRAR escorts MICK over to the chairs. He sits down.
LADY REGISTRAR: Will you take a chair, please? Your full name, please, sir?
MICK: Michael Arnold Travis.
LADY REGISTRAR: And yours, madam?
OLD LADY: Elizabeth Valerie Stewart.
The REGISTRAR turns to the MALE NURSE who scrawls their names on to white labels with a chinagraph pencil.
The OLD LADY whispers to MICK.
OLD LADY: How much are they paying you?
MICK (loudly): One hundred and fifty pounds.
OLD LADY: I'm getting seventy five and all the food I can eat.

REGISTRAR: Professor Millar will be with you in a minute.
She hangs the white cards around their necks.
A cluster of doctors, white-coated, holding files, brief-cases and clipboards, walk briskly into the hall. In the centre of them is PROFESSOR MILLAR, tall, authoritative, with thinning red hair and the piercing eye of the true obsessive.
PROFESSOR MILLAR: That's a distinct improvement, Ross... (calling to the man in front): ... Oh, Doctor Bee!
BEE (turning): Sir?
MICK looks at them.
MILLAR: I'll be coming into your Department at eleven. I'll want Mrs Unwin under the Pathoscope. We may have to remodel her transplant.
The doctors twitter with excitement.
BEE: Certainly, sir.
MILLAR: How long is it now?
BEE: Three hundred and fifty seven days.
MILLAR: Fraenkel in Boston kept one surviving for fourteen months. I'd like to beat him.
General laughter.
ANOTHER DOCTOR: You will, sir!
LADY DOCTOR: Professor Millar....
MILLAR: One moment, Houston...
The MALE NURSE from the car approaches the group.
MALE NURSE: The new intake is ready, Professor.
MILLAR: Ah—splendid—
PROFESSOR MILLAR steps forward briskly. The LADY DOCTOR chases after him and speaks to him as he inspects the OLD LADY's name card.
LADY DOCTOR: Oh, Professor Millar—can I borrow a heart from the organ bank for three days?
MILLAR (inspecting the OLD LADY's card): I'll have to come back to you on that one, Houston—we may need everything we've got this week....
HOUSTON withdraws. PROFESSOR MILLAR shakes the OLD LADY by the hand and moves on to MICK.
LADY DOCTOR: Very well.
MILLAR (to the OLD LADY): Delighted to have you here. (He moves on): I'm Professor Millar. (He inspects MICK's card).
MICK: How do you do, sir.
MILLAR: Do sit down: Excuse me.... (He leans forward and pulls

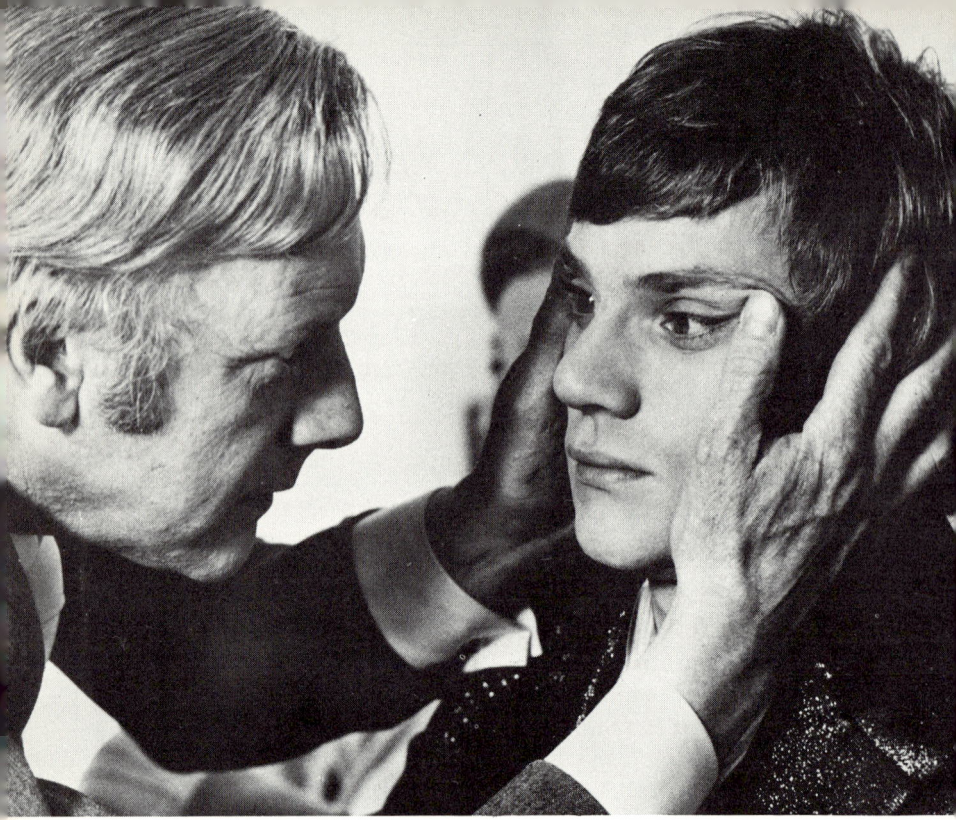

MICK's eyelids with his thumbs): Mmm. . . . . Interesting. Good. I'm delighted to have you here. I'll see you both later. Sister Hallett, room Nine for Mr Travis and Thirty Six for Mrs Stewart. I'll want a complete analysis on Travis by this afternoon.
SISTER HALLETT: Yes, Professor.
  PROFESSOR MILLAR sweeps on. SISTER HALLETT calls briefly.
SISTER HALLETT: Hughes—Keating.
  The two porters pocket their papers and each takes a wheelchair.

LIFTS
  The porters wheel MICK and the OLD LADY to the lifts. The right-hand lift is open. HUGHES swings the OLD LADY's chair round and draws it into the lift. She waves and smiles to MICK, who crosses his legs and waves back as the doors close. KEATING pushes MICK's chair into the other lift. Inside the lift, MICK watches KEATING do the crossword.

CLINIC CORRIDORS
  KEATING wheels MICK out of the lift and along the corridor.

They pass a man in a dressing gown, hobbling on crutches. A covered form is transported on a wheeled trolley. A nurse watches MICK closely as he is wheeled in to a room whose door is inscribed: 'ANALYSIS ROOM'.

ANALYSIS ROOM
MICK is now stripped down and wearing only surgical pants, sitting up on a reclining hospital couch. Around him, on benches and tables and in tall metal cabinets, are the various apparati for testing and recording—TV screens, encephalograph, radiograph, clocks measuring minutes and seconds, computers, electronic recorders.
NURSE HALLETT is arranging MICK's clothes (including his gold suit) on a hanger. A DOCTOR is taping electrodes to MICK's head. These wire him to the television screen of an encephalograph. A SECOND DOCTOR is standing near the foot of the couch with a clipboard and a pen, recording MICK's details.
SECOND DOCTOR: Feeling comfortable?
MICK: Yes, sir. Thank you. Fine.

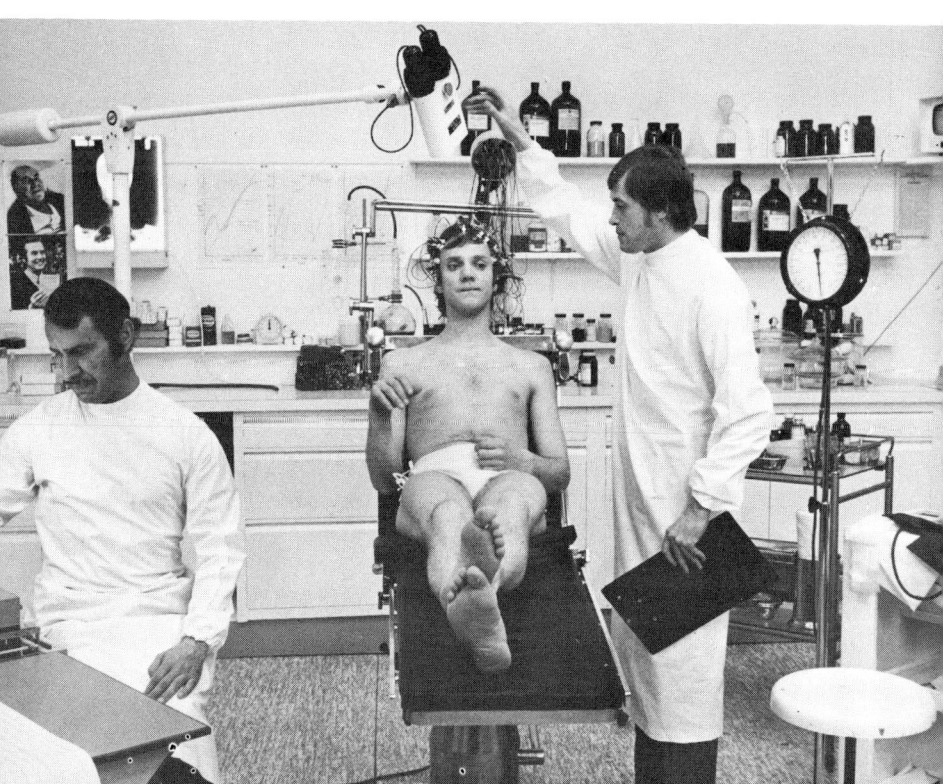

Second Doctor: Waterworks OK?
Mick: Yes, fine, thank you.
> The First Doctor is turning switches, producing low electtronic hums.

Second Doctor (taking notes): No inherent madness in the family?
Mick: None whatsoever... Hey, where's she taking my suit?
> Nurse Hallett is leaving the room with Mick's clothes on the hanger.

Nurse Hallett: Don't worry you'll find it in your wardrobe.
> The First Doctor moves round to attach electrodes to Mick's wrist.

First Doctor: Just flex your wrist.
Second Doctor: And you've never seen insects crawling up the walls... No fits?
Mick: Uh... No—never.
> The First Doctor has moved back now to his machine.

First Doctor: Ready when you are, Stanley....
Second Doctor (finishing off): No typhoid... cholera... epilepsy... The usual jabs at childhood.
> Mick nods. The Doctor finishes his notes and crosses to join the First Doctor at the encephalograph.

First Doctor: Right—here we go.
> He turns a switch. The machine produces further electronic noises, and needles leap to life. Mick tenses expectantly.

First Doctor: Hello—E.X. at 82 per cent!
Second Doctor: Are you sure?
> Mick glances apprehensively over at the machine.

First Doctor: Have a look. Frontal circuit at 7.4, rear lobes neutral.
Second Doctor: Step it up a bit... (a pause: further noises)... J.M. will be happy about this.

> Professor Millar enters, urgency well under control. Mick is now completely wired up, so that electrical impulses may be read from all parts of his body. The Second Doctor hands Millar the clipboard notes to read. The First Doctor is reading the needle indications on the various dials. From time to time he makes an adjustment on one of the various connections to Mick's limbs.

Millar (gravely): Michael, I don't know if anyone's ever told you this, but you happen to belong to a very rare group of encephaloids.

MICK: What's that supposed to mean?
MILLAR: Essentially it means that you are in a position to be particularly helpful to us in our research.
MICK: What kind of research?
MILLAR: What do you think is the most successful animal that's ever lived on this earth?
MICK: The Ant?
MILLAR: The Dinosaur.

    ANALYSIS ROOM   SECOND STAGE
    MICK is sandwiched between two stretchers on a revolving wheel-like bed, still wired-up. He moves with the arc of the machine as it revolves, anti-clockwise. PROFESSOR MILLAR is talking urgently and persuasively.
MILLAR: Do you realise that the Dinosaur dominated this globe for 140 million years before they became extinct? Man has been on this planet for only a fraction over 40,000 years—and yet already he faces extinction. In fact, the species will be lucky to survive beyond the year two thousand and ten. Mankind has only one hope. Science. "Technology is the survival kit of the human race." Even

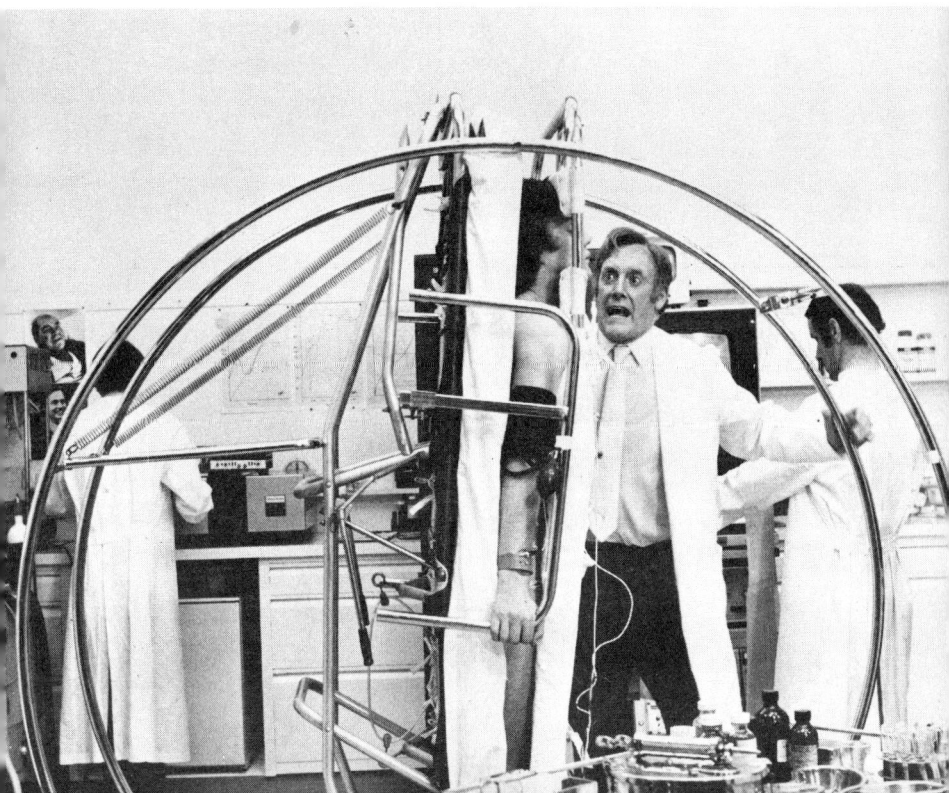

the politicians realise this. What they don't—or won't—realise is that the technical solutions are already within our power. The entire population of India could be re-housed on the moon within ten years. It's only a matter of learning to live in a new way.

ANALYSIS ROOM   THIRD STAGE
MICK is on an exercise bicycle with a breathing tube in his mouth and a clip on his nose. Various other wires are attached to his head. The FIRST DOCTOR operates the switch, adjusting the position etc. while the SECOND DOCTOR examines something in the background. As PROFESSOR MILLAR continues to lecture, MICK pedals furiously.

MILLAR: You could have 500 million people living perfectly comfortably in the British Isles, granted an intelligent adaptation of the battery system. We only have to enclose and drain the Irish Sea and the English Channel, and we could increase our manpower to 800 million by the end of the century. There's no real limit to the population this island could contain. No human being really needs more than $7\frac{1}{2}$ square feet to lead a fully functional existence.

PROFESSOR MILLAR re-adjusts the nose clip.

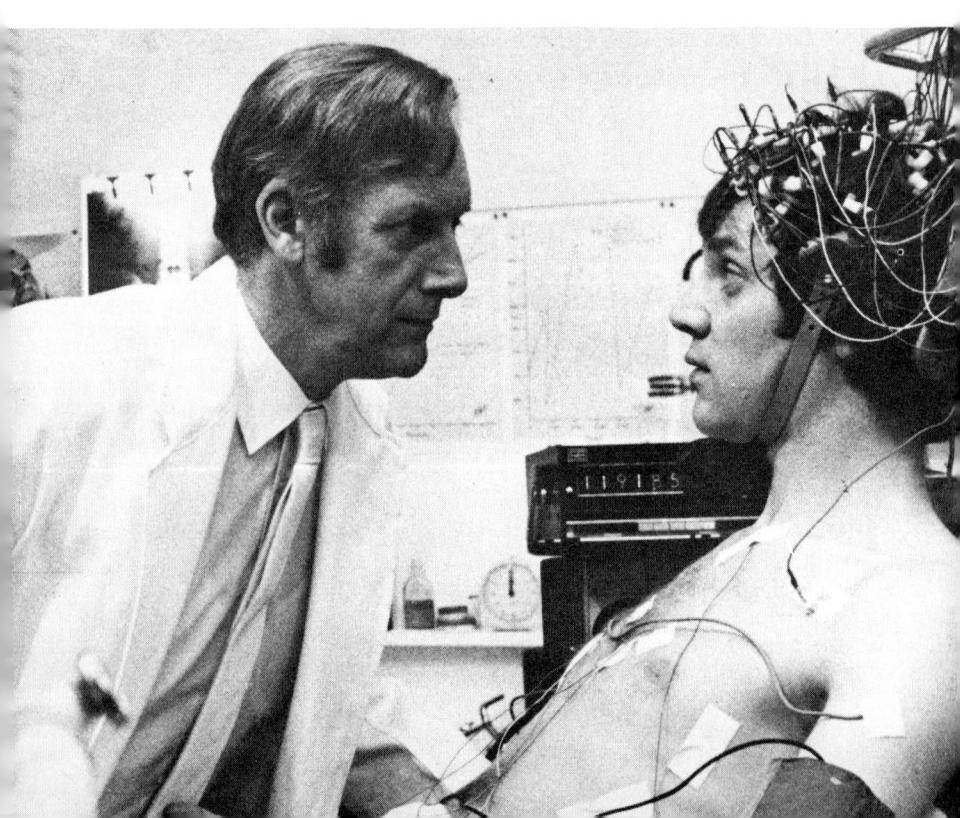

ANALYSIS ROOM   FOURTH STAGE
>   MICK is horizontal again, with wires taped to his stomach, legs, arms and neck. His hand is enclosed in a vacuum-sealed transparent plastic container, filled with green liquid. Wires run from this container to a pressure gauge, whose readings are being noted by the FIRST DOCTOR. The SECOND DOCTOR is adjusting the terminals. PROFESSOR MILLAR continues to speak, leaning over MICK.

FIRST DOCTOR: Absolutely still.

MILLAR: We have almost conquered the concept of disease. With present transplant techniques there is no reason why everyone shouldn't live to be 250 or 300 years old, instead of our present miserable 70 or 80 years.

>   PROFESSOR MILLAR moves closer to MICK.

MILLAR: We are on the verge of a whole series of discoveries that will transform our conception of human life...

MICK'S ROOM

MICK: What's all this got to do with me?

>   MICK is now in bed. His room is bare except for a table, wardrobe, chair, and a reproduction of Constable's 'Cornfield' on the white wall. PROFESSOR MILLAR is standing at his bedside. He speaks with intensity. Transported, PROFESSOR MILLAR paces the floor. SISTER HALLETT sits by the table. MICK has an apple.

MILLAR: Michael, at this very moment, in laboratories throughout the world, life is being created.

>   MICK polishes his apple and then takes a bite.

MILLAR: It's only a matter of years—perhaps even months—before we can begin to produce a whole generation of new and far more fully adapted creatures. I have a Mongol in the experimental wing here who can't tie his own shoe-laces. By the end of the summer he will be a contract bridge champion... Falling in love, making love—we'll no longer need to depend on this absurdly inefficient way of distributing random genes. Computers, programmed to select the correctly matched DNA molecules, will be able to produce an entirely satisfactory human breed. This is the future, Michael. This is the work for which I need your help.

MICK: Yes, but what's going to happen to me? Will I come out the same as I went in?

MILLAR: Not the same—better! (taking a folder from the NURSE):

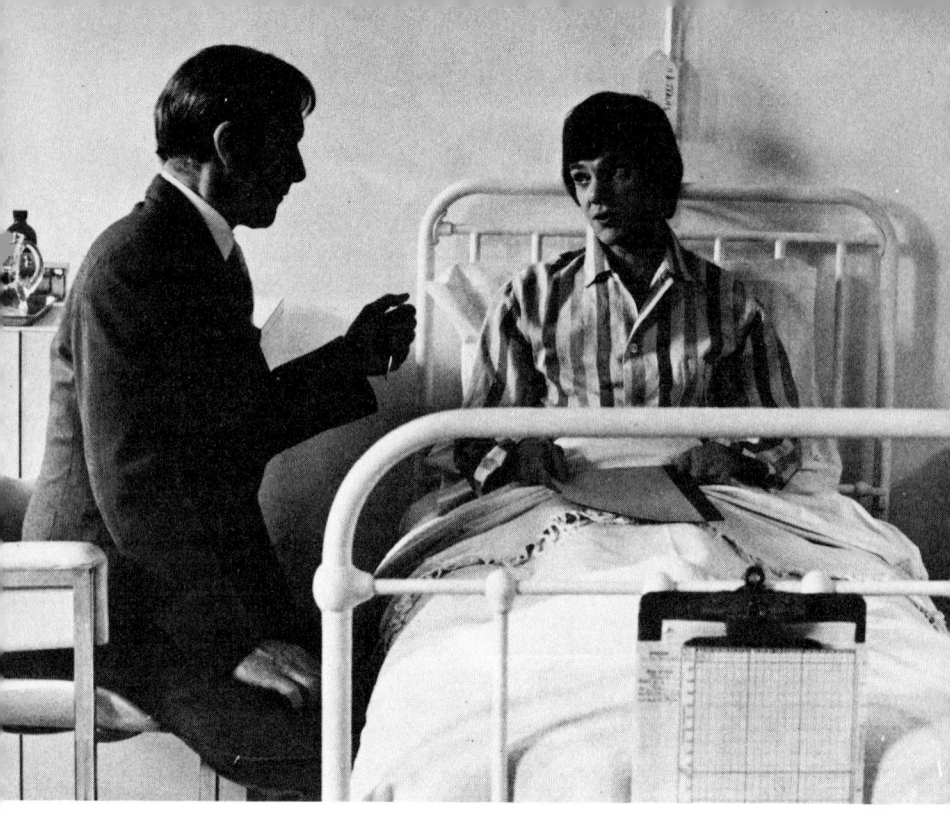

Now, I'd just like you to sign this release form.
> He sits at MICK's bedside. MICK takes the folder, but not the pen which the PROFESSOR holds out to him. He starts to read:

MICK: .... "I hereby consent to lease the Millar Research Clinic all physical experimental rights in my body for one week for the sum of One Hundred Pounds." Well, I'd like to help, Professor Millar, but a hundred and fifty pounds is definitely my minimum price. Definitely.
> He tosses the folder back onto the bed.

MILLAR: A figure like that is just beyond us.
MICK: £150. I'm not going to argue about it.
MILLAR: £130.
MICK: £145.
MILLAR: £135.
MICK: £140.
MILLAR: Done! Sign by the cross.
> He holds out his pen. MICK takes it and signs. The PROFESSOR rises.

MILLAR: Sister Hallett.
SISTER: Yes, Professor.

MILLAR : Give Mr Travis a sedative.
SISTER : Certainly.
MILLAR : Sleep well, Michael.
> PROFESSOR MILLAR leaves the room as NURSE HALLETT pours water into a glass and brings it to MICK with a green and red pill. MICK smiles, pleased at the success of his bargaining, and swallows the pill.

> It is now dark in MICK'S room : a blue light burns in the ceiling. PROFESSOR MILLAR is standing at the foot of the bed, talking in a low voice to NURSE HALLETT as the camera pans over MICK'S sleeping body.

MILLAR : All quiet?
NURSE HALLETT : Yes, Professor.
MILLAR : No fluctuations?
NURSE HALLETT : Quite stable.
MILLAR : I'll take him first. It'll be a long job. Four or five hours.
NURSE HALLETT : Do you think it'll take, Professor?
MILLAR : Mm. . . . There's an even chance. He's in reasonably good condition.
NURSE : Oh, yes.
MILLAR : Is he sterilised yet?
NURSE HALLETT : Not yet, Professor.
MILLAR : You'd better send for Doctor Bee.
NURSE : Yes, Professor.
> PROFESSOR MILLAR tiptoes from the room. NURSE HALLETT stands for a moment looking down at MICK. She gives a little smile and touches his hair back from his forehead. Then she leaves the room.

> MICK opens his eyes. He sits up, listening. He gets out of bed and goes to the door. Cautiously he opens it. Peers out.

> The corridor is empty. MICK leans round and sees a card fixed on a wall beside his door : 'DNA EXPERIMENTAL PRO-GRAMME PROFESSOR MILLAR'S SUBJECT TRAVIS. M.A. FOR SURGERY'. MICK glances round again, then slips back into his room. The camera moves in to the card.

> MICK stealthily leaves his room wearing the gold suit over his pyjamas. The corridor is still empty. He tiptoes along. Suddenly he hears approaching voices. He retreats to a doorway. The

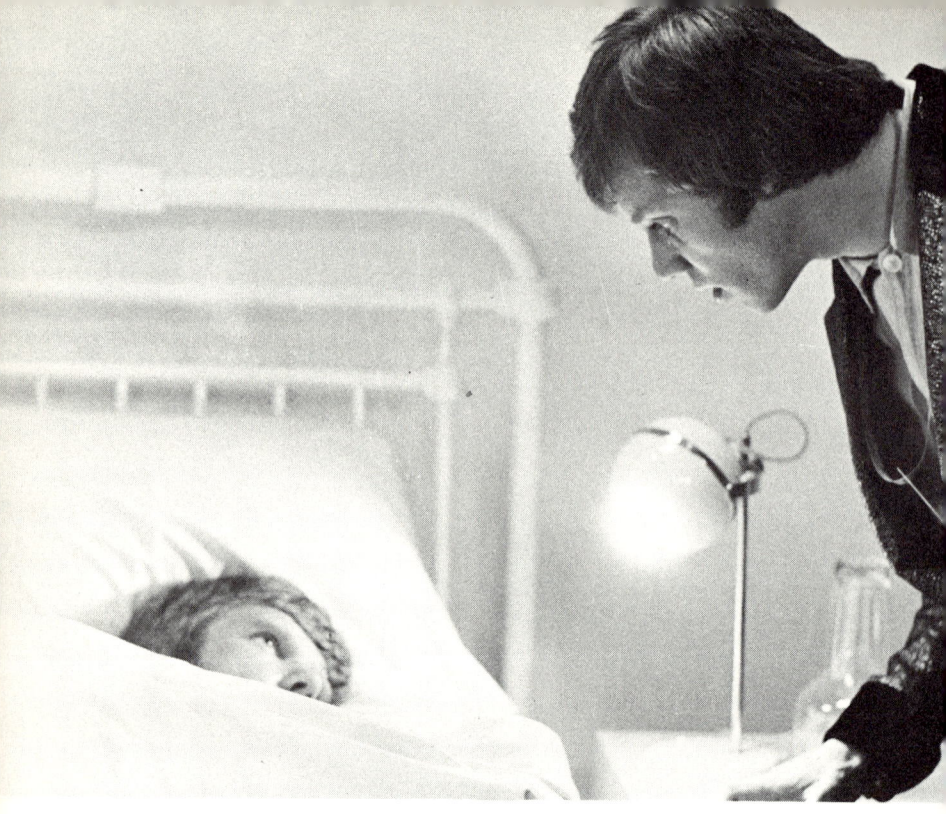

Male Nurse and the Night Sister enter the corridor, chatting together.
Sister: Now, Professor Bee's new patient will require two injections during the night. One at twelve and one at four. Is that understood?
Male Nurse: Yes, sister.
  The Male Nurse walks on down the corridor. As he draws nearer, Mick finds the door open behind him and slips into the dark room.

BEDROOM
  A room like Mick's bedroom, illuminated only by a blue night light. There is the sound of whimpering.
Mick: Sssh. It's all right. Sssh...
  Mick tiptoes towards the bed. In it is a Young Man. Mick comes closer and peers down at him.
Mick: How much are they paying you?
  The Young Man whimpers and moves his head restlessly. Mick switches the bedside lamp on. The Young Man's movements become more agitated: it is as though he is in pain.

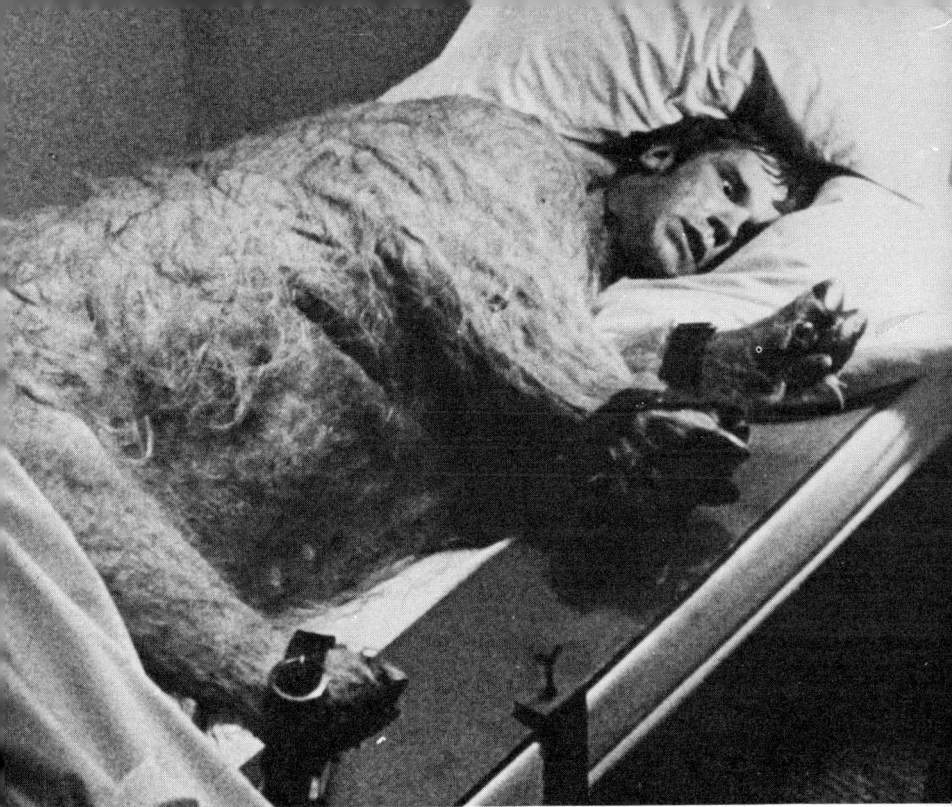

Mick draws back the bedclothes. He sees something strange. He rips the sheet back. He screams and starts back. The Young Man's head is grafted to the body of a large pig. The hooves are strapped down to a wooden frame. Mick flees in terror. The Pig-Boy threshes convulsively.

CORRIDOR
Mick rushes out of the room, towards the lift. It opens and he turns and runs back down the corridor. He collides with a nurse and sends her flying. At the end is a big window; Mick dives through it head first.

THE CLINIC FACADE
A slow-motion explosion of glass. Mick flies out of the window into space.
The lights come on in the windows of the Clinic. Doctors and nurses run out. Dogs bark.

THE CLINIC GATE
It is very dark. Mick, now on a bicycle, races out through the

Clinic gates. He turns the corner onto a country road and belts down it.

Headlights from an approaching vehicle flare into his eyes. He swerves violently: the vehicle skids to avoid him: MICK is precipitated into a ditch at the side of the road.

The vehicle, a white minibus, skids across the road, knocks the MILLAR CLINIC sign to the ground and comes to a stop on the grass verge. The driver—the ROADIE—jumps out of the van.

ROADIE : Hello! . . Is there anybody there?

MICK climbs out of the ditch, soaked from head to foot.

MICK : For Christ's sake. . . . You could have killed me! Why don't you look where you're going?

ROADIE : Are you all right?

The middle door of the van opens and there is a shout. A figure leans out. It is ALAN.

ALAN : Hey! . . Cut the conference!

MICK : Look at my bloody suit.

MICK stumbles forward to the van.

ALAN (to MICK as he approaches): Are you suing us—or are we suing you?

MICK : Going to London?

ALAN : Yeah—we *were*.

MICK : Can you give us a lift? OK?

ALAN looks into the van a moment, then tugs the sliding door wide open to let him in.

ALAN : Yeah. Come on. Get in. . .

INSIDE THE VAN

MICK climbs in. ALAN leans across and closes the door.

ALAN : Sit in the back there and keep your mouth shut.

TOLLY and DAVE are playing chess at the table. ALAN sits with them, a bottle of whisky on the table in front of him. COLIN is next to TOLLY, watching the game.

TOLLY : Oh, it's the Golden Wonder.

MICK glances round then sits down on the back seat.

The ROADIE climbs back into the driving seat.

ALAN (taking a swig of whisky): C'mon Streaky. Let's aggravate the gravel.

The van drives off.

BLACKOUT

Inside the van. Silence. Occasionally lights flicker past the curtained windows, and there is the sound of a passing car. MICK looks round at the chess players. The game is going slowly.

ALAN: If you don't take that castle soon, the National Trust will.
    TOLLY lifts a hand as though to make a move; then lowers his hand again; and continues to stare at the board.
    MICK's attention is drawn to the seat beside him. Under a fur coat something is moving. He glances at ALAN. ALAN looks back, giving nothing away. MICK pulls back the fur coat. A girl's face, upside down. She rights herself, looking up at him. She likes what she sees. She sits up, pulling a rug around her. She is a sensuous, rather *louche* blonde. She speaks with a confident upper-class accent. ALAN continues to watch.
PATRICIA: You're shivering.
MICK: I'm wet.
PATRICIA: Take off that jacket.
    MICK hesitates, then wriggles out of his jacket. PATRICIA finds a plastic bag. She feels his wet pyjama top.
PATRICIA: And that.
    MICK takes off the pyjama jacket. He clasps his arms round his shoulders, shivering.
PATRICIA: Alan—pass us the rug. And the bottle. (to MICK): Take off your trousers. . . . Come on, strip off.
MICK: What? Here?
    ALAN comes over with the rug and the whisky bottle.
ALAN: Get them off. This is Patricia. She's very intelligent. She's making a study of us.
    PATRICIA smiles, then passes MICK the bottle.
MICK (before drinking): Thank you.
    She takes the crumpled rug and wraps it round him. MICK starts to undo his trousers.
MICK: What are you? What do you do?
PATRICIA: They're musicians.
TOLLY: We just try to make some bread—that's all, mate.
MICK: Are you rich?
ALAN: No, but me manager is.
    ALAN takes a swig.
    The van drives on down the dark road.
    MICK pulls his trousers off from under the rug, and hands them to PATRICIA.

Mick: Be careful of those... That's gold thread.
Patricia (inspecting them): Nylon.
   She puts them in a plastic bag.
Tolly: Check-mate, Dave.
Alan: Never mind. At least you got it wrong.
   Alan climbs forward to sit with the Roadie.

The van passes a huge floodlit sign on the motorway. It reads: 'THE SOUTH LONDON NOTTINGHAM'.

Mick and Patricia are sitting apart in the back of the van.
Patricia: Come over here.
   Mick slides over right next to her. Patricia studies his face. After a moment she lifts an arm and puts it round him. She licks her fingers, wetting them, and tries to clean the dirt off his face. She leans towards him and kisses his neck. Then she draws back. Mick looks at her, then leans forward and kisses her. They slide down on the seat. Mick's arm comes over and encircles her. They make love.

The van drives on.

Colin, Tolly and Dave sleep round the table. Alan glances round. He sees Mick and Patricia and smiles.
Alan (to the Roadie): Waifs and strays—she never could resist.

The van drives on down the central carriageway, overtaken by the occasional fast car or racing lorry-driver.

Mick cradles Patricia in his arms. They are both asleep.

Outskirts of London.

Mick opens his eyes and sees that they are now on a city flyover. Gently he disentangles himself, and makes his way forward to Alan, past the sleeping musicians. Music begins.
Mick: How long?
Alan: About an hour. Maybe less.
   Alan yawns. Mick leans over the front passenger seat near Alan. Alan offers him a polo mint. Mick takes one. He peers through the front window.

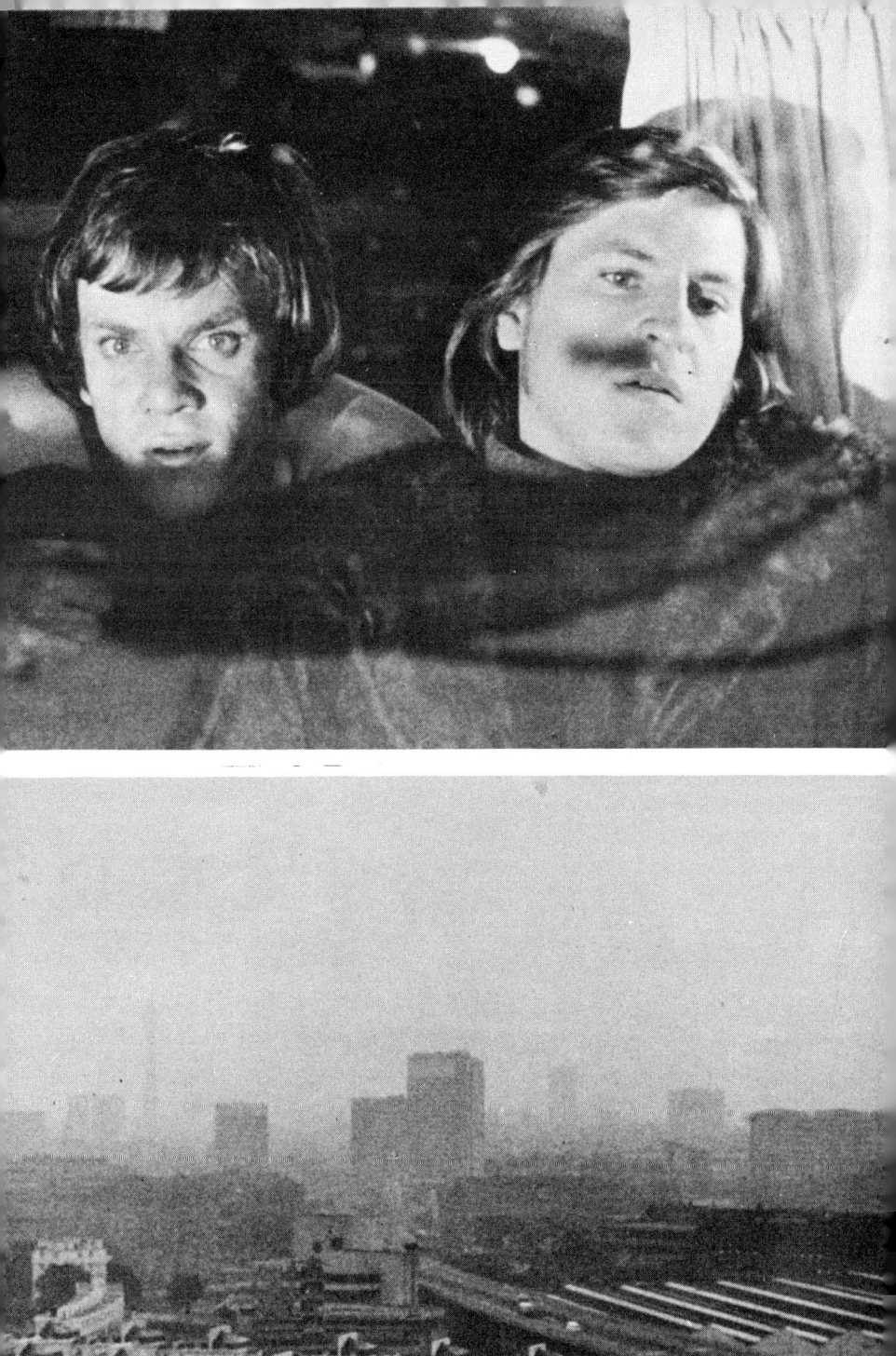

110

The road stretches ahead. Morning is in the sky.

MICK watches the road, the sky, the buildings. His eyes are wide.

From high up, looking down on to the motorway leading into the city, the camera pans to follow the van as it heads into London.
The city of London, the warehouses, the new office blocks, the factories and the houses of London's ten million people. All in the pale mist of early morning.
BLACKOUT

TITLE : *SOUTH*

PATRICIA'S BEDROOM
A large room with a double bed at one end and near it a chest of drawers. One wall is lined with cupboards with sliding doors. Old suitcases, electronic equipment and piles of newspapers are stacked against the wall. On the chest of drawers a portable

colour television, and on the wall above an unframed Renoir. Sunlight filters in through thin cotton curtains. Near the window is a dressing table with a mirror, make-up and a wig on a plastic model head.
MICK is drowsing in the large bed. He stirs and rolls over, stretching his arms out over the other side of the bed—but there is no one there. He opens his eyes, lifts himself up on his elbow and looks around. There is the sound of music playing. MICK gets out of bed and crosses the room. He opens the bedroom door curiously. Listens. ALAN's voice comes into the music: '... *On and on and on and on we go.* ...' MICK turns back into the room and pulls a mustard-coloured polo neck jersey out of the wardrobe. He throws his gold suit off the dressing-table chair and strips off his pyjama top.

REHEARSAL ROOM
A large room which may recall the limbo setting in which we have seen the group performing so far. But these walls are a grubby yellow-brown, and ALAN and the group are rehearsing in daylight.

ALAN (singing):
If you have a friend on whom you think you can rely—
You are a lucky man!
If you have a reason to live on and not to die. . . . .

A glass door opens and MICK comes in, now wearing the yellow jersey under the gold suit. He looks around, then comes over to ALAN.

MICK: Where's Patricia?
ALAN (continuing to play): She's upstairs. . . . (He points to the corner of the room): Upstairs!

MICK picks up a biscuit and pops it in his mouth. He crosses the room jauntily. The ROADIE, who is busy with an amplifier, gestures to a small staircase in the corner. MICK starts to climb.

ROOFTOP
MICK appears at the head of the stairs and pushes his way through a shabby door. He finds himself on the rooftop, an open area broken by chimney stacks and a skylight. He looks over the edge—a vista of rooftops and railway lines. He looks round and sees PATRICIA at the other end of the roof. She is painting on a chimney stack, on which already there is in-

scribed a formalised tree-design. She stands on a ladder holding a book in one hand. She wears a voile dress. MICK looks round, then bounces over to her and kisses her.

MICK: Morning.
PATRICIA: How do you feel?
MICK: Hungry.
PATRICIA (giving him the book): Could you hold this for me?
MICK takes the book and studies the page. PATRICIA finishes the symbol.
MICK: What is it?
PATRICIA: *OM*. It means infinity or Godhead.
She comes down the ladder.
MICK: Are you a Buddhist?
PATRICIA: All religions are equally true. (She kisses him): Breakfast.....

PATRICIA claps her hands and crosses the roof to a large refrigerator, standing in the corner. She opens it and takes out a bottle of champagne, two glasses and a grapefruit. MICK walks to the edge of the roof and looks out.

MICK: London... the biggest money market in the world. Did you know that? Ten thousand million pounds a day turnover... ten thousand millions a day.... And there's a thousand ways of making it, you know. (Looking towards PATRICIA): It's just a question of picking the right one.
PATRICIA (crossing back to a table in the middle of the roof): Open this....

She tosses the grapefruit as MICK comes over to open the champagne.

MICK (looking at the bottle): Champagne!
PATRICIA (amused): Of course...
MICK (looking at the skyline): Glass palaces. Just look at them! One day I'll own one of those.
PATRICIA: You're very old-fashioned.

The champagne cork flies out. The champagne froths down the bottle. MICK fills PATRICIA's glass.

MICK: What do you mean I'm 'old-fashioned'?
PATRICIA: But all this stuff about money, and owning things... if you want something, just take it. I always do.

PATRICIA moves away to a chair. She sits down.

MICK (referring to the Champagne): Where d'you get this from?
PATRICIA: Home.

MICK : Do you go there often?
PATRICIA : Sometimes. When I get bored.
MICK (indicating the statues and rocking horse): And where does all this other stuff come from?
PATRICIA : That comes from home too. Daddy's got so much he never misses anything.
MICK (from the edge of the roof again): You're lucky. I've got to get there on my own.
PATRICIA : Get where?
MICK : Right to the top.
   MICK looks out over the city, which is dominated by a looming glass skyscraper.
MICK : How much is a building like that worth?
   PATRICIA comes and stands beside him.
PATRICIA : The ground rent is £800,000 a year. It cost ten times that to build and every three months its value increases by 20 per cent.
MICK : How do you know?
PATRICIA (slyly) : My father owns it.
MICK : Really! It's beautiful. . . . I'd like to meet your father.
PATRICIA : You've got lovely eyes. . . .
MICK : Introduce us then. I've been a top salesman earned £100 one week.
PATRICIA (laughs) : You're so greedy. . .
MICK (as PATRICIA kisses him) : Tell me more about your father.
PATRICIA (kissing him): He owns half the copper mines in the world. . . (kissing him) : For every £5 million pounds he invests, he makes fifty million pounds profit. . . (kissing him) : In Bolivia he drove half a million peasants off their land. (On these words the camera moves in on the tallest glass building.) They starved to death. . . . (She kisses him.)
MICK (rapt) : 50 million pounds profit! . . .
PATRICIA (licking his ear) : He's the most evil man you could ever hope to meet.
      There is a whistle. ALAN is in the street below in his cap and fur coat : he, the Roadie and one of the group are standing by the van.
ALAN (whistling again) : Are you coming or staying?
PATRICIA (looks down to the street) : Coming!
   She makes for the door.
MICK : Hey, where are you going? Don't go. . .

PATRICIA (coming back to MICK): Have a good day. Remember...
all that glisters is not gold.
PATRICIA walks away, turns a moment and waves goodbye. She vanishes. MICK watches after her, then turns away from the closed door to look out at the skyscraper. He raises his glass. The soft, rhythmic introduction to *Poor People* comes in as the camera zooms in to the glass building.

PATRICIA'S BEDROOM
ALAN's voice is heard singing *Poor People*.
ALAN (singing): *Poor people are poor people—*
They don't understand
A man's got to make whatever he wants—
Take it with his own hands.

Poor people stay poor people—
They never get to see
Someone's got to win in the human race—
If it isn't you then it has to be me...

MICK comes in. He walks across the room and pulls open the bedside chest of drawers. He looks quickly through the papers and oddments till he comes across a small address book. On the flyleaf is written PATRICIA's name and home address. He thumbs through and finds the address he is looking for.
MICK: Daddy!
He picks up the phone and dials. While he waits, he closely examines the Renoir on the wall.
MICK: Hello... Can I speak to Mr Burgess, please?... Oh yes, yes, of course—Sir James... Yes... It's about his daughter. Yes, it's very urgent. I'm sorry but it's absolutely confidential. It's a matter of life and death. Well, you'll just have to interrupt him then, won't you?
As MICK waits to be put through, he crosses the room, still holding the phone on its long extension cord, his attention caught by the long open wardrobe. PATRICIA's and ALAN's clothes are hanging side by side. MICK selects a suit. As he speaks he pulls out a shirt and tie as well, and arranges them on the back of a chair.
MICK: Hello, Sir James. Hello. I'm Michael Travis. It's about Patricia. She's in trouble. Well, she's safe at the moment, but I'm not sure how long it can be guaranteed. No.... Sir James, I really

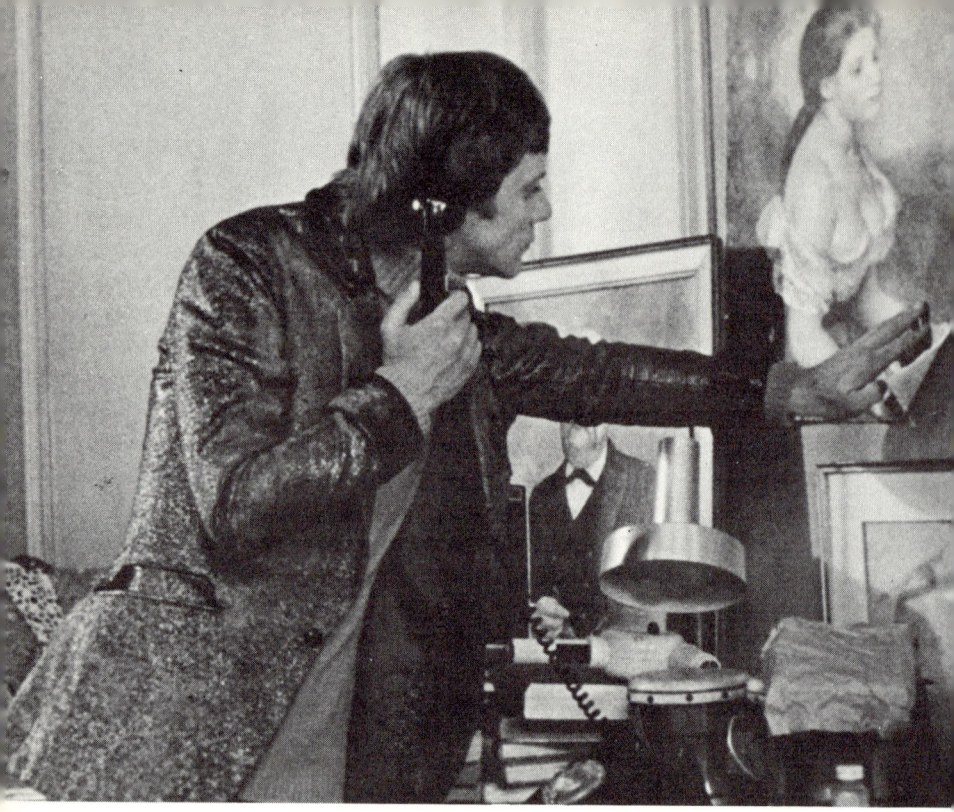

cannot discuss this on the telephone. I'm sure you understand. Well I do have rather a full afternoon, but I could see you in say . . . 45 minutes. . . No, Sir James, I'm not a psychiatrist. . . Good. Oh by the way, Sir James, which is your nearest tube station? Thank you.

    He hangs up the telephone and starts to change. The song continues. . .

ALAN (singing): *Just get out there*
                 and do it!

TOTTENHAM COURT ROAD

    MICK emerges from a tube station, looks around, and walks briskly along the crowded pavement. He stops at a crossing. The traffic stops and he crosses.

ALAN (singing): *So sing and they'll sing your song—*
                Laugh while you're getting on—
                Smile and they'll string along—
                Nobody's gonna know.

As he reaches an island in the middle of the road, he pauses, straightens his tie and looks up at the glass building.

The camera tilts slowly up the full height of the building.

TOP FLOOR OFFICE SUITE

MICK emerges from the lift. A welcoming SECRETARY rises from her desk to meet him as the lift doors open. The decor is severe —in black, white and chrome.

SECRETARY: Mr Travis? Would you mind taking a seat and waiting a few moments. Sir James is still in conference.

MICK sits in a leather chair and looks around. The SECRETARY walks back to her desk. He smiles at the SECRETARY. She smiles back. MICK hears voices raised in anger from the other side of a pair of elegant black doors: the sound of violent argument.

PROFESSOR STEWART (off-screen, urgent): It's only a question of time... Another six months is all I need...

SIR JAMES (off-screen): No!

PROFESSOR STEWART (off-screen): Please!

SIR JAMES (off-screen): Impossible....

The SECRETARY smiles again at MICK. He smiles back. STEWART suddenly screams...

PROFESSOR STEWART (screaming): No—No—No—you rotten bastard! You swine! Can't you see it's a revolutionary concept!

The doors open and a dapper young man—WILLIAM (SIR JAMES' Personal Assistant)—firmly ushers a distraught, wild-eyed PROFESSOR out of the room. PROFESSOR STEWART wears a crumpled tweed jacket, an old check shirt and a wool tie.

PROFESSOR STEWART (sobbing): 25 years of my life. 25 years wasted. 25 years down the drain. Oh God—all wasted—

WILLIAM escorts PROFESSOR STEWART past the SECRETARY's desk. She is typing and pretends not to notice. Suddenly PROFESSOR STEWART runs back into the room.

PROFESSOR STEWART: You bastard! You swine!

WILLIAM rushes after him and drags him out of the room. SIR JAMES is glimpsed through the door at his desk. MICK and the SECRETARY ignore the hysterical PROFESSOR.

As they near the lift, PROFESSOR STEWART lunges out and suddenly grabs hold of MICK's leg. MICK is dragged to the floor.

PROFESSOR STEWART (imploring): Help me. I won't go. I'll never go. Don't let them do it.

SIR JAMES appears in the door, implacably authoritative.

SIR JAMES: Miss Hunter—two valium and a barley wine for Professor Stewart, please. William—a chair for Professor Stewart.

SIR JAMES vanishes back into his office.

WILLIAM and MICK help PROFESSOR STEWART into a chair. He is sobbing. The SECRETARY (Miss Hunter) reaches into a cupboard behind her desk and brings out a bottle of barley wine. She carries it across to the PROFESSOR. WILLIAM crosses to SIR JAMES' door and speaks for a moment, then he turns and approaches MICK. He speaks in cool, clipped tones.

WILLIAM: Mr Travis, Sir James' time is worth £500 per minute. Please keep it short.

MICK follows him, straightening his tie.

SIR JAMES' OFFICE

The office is spacious and light. SIR JAMES is at his desk, on which is a small stone sculpture and a small silver tray with tea-things. A modern black-and-white abstract hangs on the wall behind him. On the facing wall is a large panoramic photograph of modern London, all business blocks and glass towers. A long, large window runs along the side wall.

WILLIAM introduces MICK from the doorway.

WILLIAM: Mr Michael Travis, Sir James.

WILLIAM disappears, closing the door behind him. A short moment of nervousness, then MICK crosses to stand in front of SIR JAMES' desk.

SIR JAMES: Well, young man?

MICK: I won't beat about the bush, sir. . . .

SIR JAMES interrupts him with a look to a chair in front of the desk. MICK breaks off, glances round him as he sits down, and plunges in again.

MICK: I won't beat about the bush, sir. It's your daughter, Patricia. She's in bad trouble.

SIR JAMES (monolithic look): What kind of trouble?

MICK: Well, sir, the usual—bad company, protest, drugs.

SIR JAMES: Oh all that. Yes. . . .

SIR JAMES looks away to his tea tray. He pours himself a cup.

MICK: I think we can save her, sir. I think she should come back to her family: a family background. Do you even know where she is, sir? It must be heartbreaking for you, Sir James.

SIR JAMES is fiddling disconcertingly with the tea things.

SIR JAMES: You amaze me.

MICK: She needs you, Sir James.

SIR JAMES (distant): How strange. The trouble is I'm so frightfully busy.

There is a noise of shouting.
PROFESSOR STEWART: No, no, I'm not going to stand for it!
The door bursts open and PROFESSOR STEWART rushes in, wild-eyed, followed by WILLIAM. SIR JAMES puts down his tea cup.
PROFESSOR STEWART: All right! If that's what you want! But here—now—in front of your very eyes, Sir James! Now!
PROFESSOR STEWART dashes to the full length window.
SIR JAMES: William! William! Stop him... at all costs!
PROFESSOR STEWART leaps up on the window seat. WILLIAM runs up and grapples with him. 'Let me go... let me go!' PROFESSOR STEWART breaks away; they scuffle; then he is back at the window, beating on the glass. Suddenly the window flies open, and both PROFESSOR STEWART and WILLIAM disappear into the void.

GLASS BUILDING
The two figures fall in a wide trajectory from the top floor of the building. The camera holds on the glass façade.

SIR JAMES' OFFICE
SIR JAMES, apalled, moves to the window. MICK peers behind SIR JAMES.

THE PAVEMENT
The two figures lie on the concrete below.

SIR JAMES' OFFICE
SIR JAMES turns and looks at MICK. Then he crosses to his desk. MICK closes the window.
SIR JAMES (into the intercom): Miss Hunter. Ask the senior staff to come to my office.
He looks at MICK again. MICK looks at him. It is an important moment. SIR JAMES goes to a bookcase and gets out a leather-bound volume. He consults the index and a relevant page.
MICK watches him warily, fixing his tie and smoothing his hair. Five senior executives enter and stand in a row facing SIR JAMES. Behind them is spread the photomural of the London skyline. Four grey, middle-aged men, one sad woman. MISS HUNTER crosses to stand beside SIR JAMES. SIR JAMES speaks solemnly.

SIR JAMES : I'm afraid I have some grave and distressing news for you. Professor Stewart is dead. Professor Stewart started life 55 years ago of humble parentage. His father was a watchmaker in Glasgow. At the age of 16 he gained a scholarship to Cambridge. During the war his vital research into the military application of electronics lead to his rapid promotion to the rank of major. (The camera and MICK study the sombre faces of the executives.) After the war he gave to this company the same loyalty that he had before given to the nation. Professor Stewart was not only an inventor of genius, but all who came in contact with him felt it a privilege to have known and loved him.
SECRETARY (looking at her watch) : Sir James. . . . it's ten past five. Your appointment with Dr Munda.
SIR JAMES : Thank you, Miss Hunter. . . . Professor Stewart was too far in advance of his time, but his name will live long. (He puts down the Company History book.) We will stand in silence in grateful memory for fifteen seconds.

> SIR JAMES stands, hands folded, eyes on watch. MICK looks at the floor and then at the executives. One of them covertly glances at his watch.

SIR JAMES : Miss Hunter, send a memo to the Chief Accountant, a gratuity of £740 per annum to his widow. Fix the funeral for Wednesday. Golders Green. And get me Vancouver.

> The SECRETARY makes a note on her pad. SIR JAMES takes his briefcase from her and gives it to MICK. MICK, surprised, follows SIR JAMES out of the office. The executives stare after them.

KNIGHTSBRIDGE
SIR JAMES' Rolls Royce drives out of an underground underpass.

SIR JAMES' ROLLS ROYCE
The Rolls is giant size. It has telephone aerials and a TV aerial. The outside world is visible through the windows. SIR JAMES and MICK recline in the rear. Two radio-telephones are fixed to the panelling.
SIR JAMES : Pity about Stewart. Brilliant man, of course, but an academic. Couldn't run a toffee shop. In business there's an animal who suceeds and an animal who doesn't. (Phone buzzes) : That may be my call to Vancouver.

> MICK answers the phone and passes it to SIR JAMES.

MICK: Vancouver, Canada, Sir James.
    SIR JAMES ignores the proferred telephone. He picks up another telephone from his side of the car.
SIR JAMES: Charles? James. I've talked to the board. Unanimous decision I'm afraid. We'll have to have your resignation by midnight. (MICK smiles.) No, two million dollars compensation is our maximum. It's your decision of course. . . but if you don't, things could be pretty upsetting for Kitty. Yes. Bye.
    SIR JAMES removes his bowler hat. He gazes out of the car.

SUBURBAN MANSION
    SIR JAMES' Rolls drives into the forecourt of a substantial detached house. A black Cadillac with diplomatic plates and a silver Audi Coupe are also parked in the drive.

MUNDA'S HOUSE   HALL
    The hall decoration is elegant. A maid has opened the front door and SIR JAMES and MICK follow her in. The maid takes SIR JAMES' hat. DR MUNDA'S tall black aide stands ready to greet them.

124

AIDE : Good evening.
SIR JAMES : Sorry to keep you. Had a little hold up at the office. . .
My assistant—Michael. . . (He looks blankly at MICK.)
MICK : Travis.
SIR JAMES : Travis.
AIDE : Morrison.
MICK : Pleased to meet you.
   They shake hands. MORRISON leads the way.
AIDE : This way, sir.

MUNDA'S LOUNGE
The atmosphere is one of cool, well-appointed good taste. Six people have been waiting, some standing, some sitting in chairs set in a semi-circle at the end of a long room. A film projector, with a slide projector set beside it, is set up behind them. Some have cups of tea in their hands, or drinks.
   DR MUNDA, a silver-haired negro—the President of Zingara—stands and comes forward to greet SIR JAMES. His tone is urbane, unctuous.
DR MUNDA : Sir James—how good of you to come.

SIR JAMES : Mr President.
  DR MUNDA introduces the people in the room. SIR JAMES shakes hands with all of them.
DR MUNDA : My Minister of Finance, Mr Timothy Souza. Madame Paillard... My Home Secretary, Mrs Naidu...
  MADAME PAILLARD is an elegant, middle-aged courtesan. MRS NAIDU is an Asian. She wears a Sari and spectacles.
DR MUNDA : Colonel Steiger.
  COLONEL STEIGER, Teutonic, with dark glasses and cropped hair, steps forward to SIR JAMES.
SIR JAMES : Ah, Colonel.
STEIGER (clicking his heels) : Sir!
DR MUNDA : Mr Oswald.
  A specious businessman in his thirties.
OSWALD : Sir James.
  MICK looks up, surprised to hear the name.
DR MUNDA : And the Right Honourable Basil Keyes, I think you know.
SIR JAMES : Basil.
BASIL KEYES (smooth) : James...
DR MUNDA : Do sit down, Sir James.
  SIR JAMES sits. The others also sit. DR MUNDA calls his AIDE forward.
DR MUNDA : Morrison—draw the curtains, please.
  MORRISON goes to the far end of the room and supervises a second manservant in the drawing of the curtains. MORRISON pulls up the projector screen himself as DR MUNDA stands in front of it. MICK crosses to sit down behind SIR JAMES. MUNDA takes the floor.
DR MUNDA : Sir James, you are a man of business. You deal in facts and figures. Well, that is what we are here to give you today.
  As DR MUNDA speaks, the maid brings SIR JAMES tea on a silver tray.
DR MUNDA : My colleagues and I are confident that we can offer you an association with our country that will be as profitable to you as to ourselves.
  MICK'S attention is attracted to OSWALD, sitting in front of him. OSWALD turns his head, sees MICK, and gives him a wink.
OSWALD : Film please, Brewster.
  MICK glances back.
  BREWSTER, a manservant sitting behind the projector, puts out

the house lights and switches on the slide projector. Lush travelogue music starts with images of blue sea, golden sands, yachts and swimming pools.

OSWALD stands to the right of the screen.

OSWALD (voice over): The coastline of Zingara. An uninterrupted stretch of golden sand, perfect for swimming, watersports and all the leisure facilities demanded by holiday makers from the industrial centres in Europe and the Americas. The island already boasts one large hotel. Visitors can take their ease in surroundings of luxury and sophistication.

A MANSERVANT comes up to SIR JAMES.

SIR JAMES: A brandy, please.

MANSERVANT: Yes, sir.

The film shows Zingaran natives prancing in ethnic displays...

OSWALD (continues, voice over): Picturesque entertainment is provided by Zingaran natives performing their age-old rituals for patrons of our holiday lodges in the hill districts. Here, in surroundings of peace and calm, staffs are being specially trained to satisfy European demands for courtesy and service.

MICK stares across at MADAME PAILLARD who is sitting beside

Dr Munda. She feels his stare and returns his look, enigmatic. Dr Munda's hand reaches out for hers and places it comfortably on his crotch.

Oswald (continues, voice over): A massive programme of hotel construction is under way. Experienced European engineers are supervising the native labour force in the construction of the Zingara Continental Hotel.

The Manservant brings Sir James his brandy.

The images have changed now to ragged Zingaran natives using picks and shovels in the dust; then hideous 'artist's impressions' of a typical international-style tourist hotel.

Oswald (continues, voice over): The completed hotel with its splendid public facilities, provides 500 rooms, each with colour television and private bathroom. . . Thank you, Brewster.

The projector is switched off. The lights come on. Oswald bows to Sir James and sits. The Zingarans applaud.

Sir James: Very attractive. But. . . your plans for industry?

Dr Munda: Our Free Export Zone will offer generous advantages to all concerns financed by foreign capital.

Sir James: Repatriation of profits?

Dr Munda : Mr Souza...
> Souza stands, picking up a large presentation folder, which he takes over and hands to Sir James.

Souza : Guaranteed to any country you care to nominate... Venezuela, the Vatican, Lichtenstein... etc.

Sir James : Oh, thanks very much.
> He passes the presentation book to Mick.

Sir James : Labour costs?

Dr Munda : Our Home Secretary, Mrs Naidu, will explain the favourable arrangements we are planning for this area.
> Mrs Naidu stands, bows to Sir James, and moves to the left of the screen.

Mrs Naidu : Labour conditions in Zingara offer excellent opportunities for the foreign investor. Rates of pay and working conditions are regulated by the Government, consequently strikes and slowdowns are a thing unknown. Film Brewster, please.
> At the mention of rates of pay, Sir James indicates to Mick to pass his briefcase : he zips it open.

> The lights go out and the film projector starts again. First a sequence of Zingaran industry : what appears to be a gum-boot factory : a tailor cutting cloth : a sausage factory. These are followed by shots of Zingaran men and women working separately, and a vast collection of white hutches—their separate living-quarters.

Mrs Naidu (voice over) : The efficiency and variety of our light industrial installations are a joy to behold. The Bumangi Sausage Factory, has a daily output of over 2,000 pounds prime first quality sausages all 75% genuine meat. Special attention is paid to cleanliness. Experience has shown that production levels benefit considerably when the sexes are segregated. Here is an ultra modern male workers' camp on the outskirts of Bikana. Their women are housed in a similar camp some 35 miles distant. Male workers are paid the equivalent of 7 new English pence per day and females at 3.
> Sir James makes a note of this. The film's images now switch to black technicians working under white supervision : white workers enjoying the 'high life' beside their swimming pools.

Mrs Naidu (voice over) : Foreign technicians are welcome in Zingara. Life for our foreign visitors and colleagues in Zingara will be fully commensurate with the standards of comfort and convenience enjoyed by their colleagues in America or the European Common Market. They will also be exempted from all personal

income tax. Thank you.
> Projector stops. House lights come on.

MRS NAIDU : Thank you, Sir James.
> She returns to her chair.

DR MUNDA : Well, Sir James, I hope we have convinced you that Zingara today presents a unique opportunity for secure investment at a high rate of return.

SIR JAMES : There is just one consideration that troubles me, Mr President.

DR MUNDA : Please. . . ?

SIR JAMES : What guarantees can you provide for the safe-guarding of investment? I refer, of course, to the threat of insurrection.
> DR MUNDA's smile fades to a look of wary concern.

DR MUNDA : Sir James, I will be completely honest.
> He gets up and walks over to stand beside SIR JAMES' chair.
> SIR JAMES' eyes flicker with mistrust.

DR MUNDA : It is true that a small element of our people have been attempting to cause unrest in our Northern Territories. This problem we have firmly in hand. We are fortunate to have secured the services of Colonel Steiger, whose achievements in the Congo, in Nigeria and more recently in Bangla Desh, must be well known to you.
> MICK looks over his shoulder. COLONEL STEIGER stands, clicks his heels, and bows to SIR JAMES.

DR MUNDA : I have asked Colonel Steiger himself to report on the situation.
> COLONEL STEIGER steps forward, and stands beside the screen. MUNDA sits. STEIGER speaks in clipped, rather high-pitched tones. His delivery is business-like, impersonal. His accent is German.

STEIGER : The rebels number roughly 2,000. Men and women. . .
Projection!
> The lights go out. The film projector starts, with first a map of Zingara, featuring animated shading and arrows, then shots of STEIGER's forces in action against the Zingaran rebels. Helicopters, tanks, machine-guns.

STEIGER (continues) : They are operating in the Northern Territories in two main groups. My counter-offensive has taken the form of a two-pronged blitz : Blanket bombardment, artillery and aircraft, followed by landings of airborne policing detachments, employing scorched earth and random elimination techniques.

SIR JAMES watches, poker-faced. Now the film shows Zingaran villages going up in flames and smoke, dead bodies littering the ground as mercenaries stand around, natives shot dead, or trussed up like chickens, or herded into a guarded compound.

STEIGER (continues): My men all professionals, experienced in guerilla warfare. The rebels are amateurs, inexperienced and weak in defence, so insurgent losses are heavy. Over 300 killed, 450 captured and interned.

The film finishes. The lights come on. DR MUNDA and MADAME PAILLARD look across to SIR JAMES. There is a slight pause.

SIR JAMES: In view of your undoubted superiority, Colonel Steiger, can you tell us why this insurrection still persists?

STEIGER stands in front of the screen.

STEIGER: The terrain is unfavourable, sir. Jungle and swamp favour the native. That is why we need *Honey*.

SIR JAMES: Honey?

STEIGER: Precisely. Your British Honey. The substance known as PL.45, or in the terminology of my profession—'Honey'. Let me show you some examples.

STEIGER steps back beside the screen. The lights go out. Slide

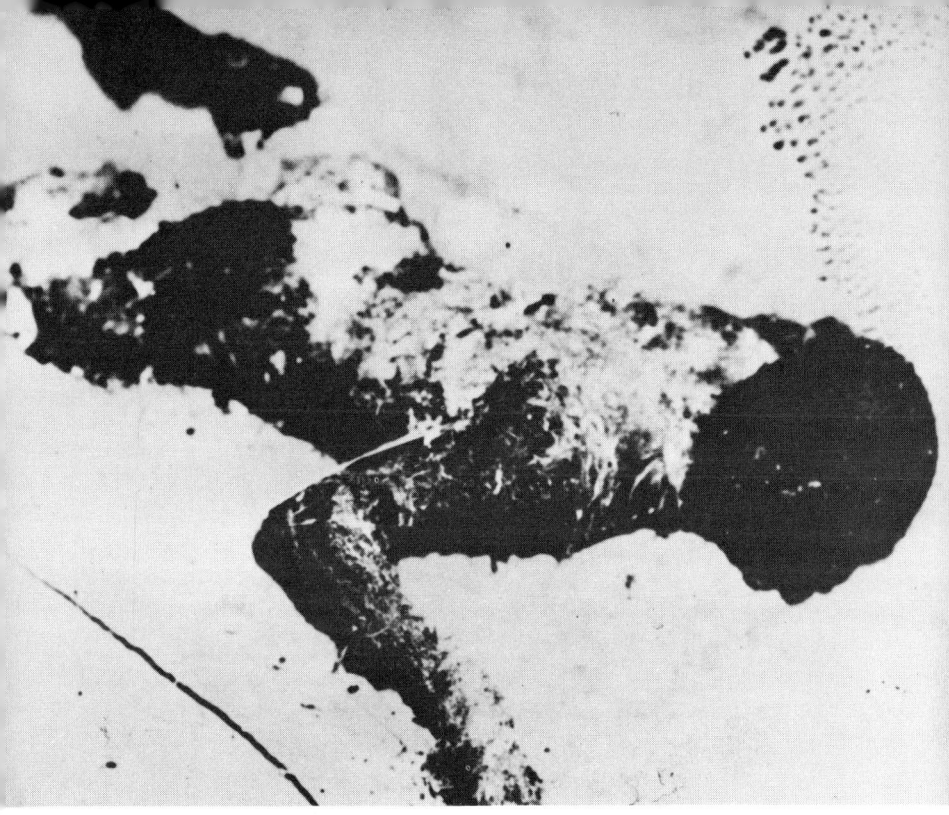

projector comes on. We see an Asian-type peasant with his face horribly scarred and burned by some Napalm-like substance.
STEIGER: This is a man who has received a light exposure to this invaluable weapon... (He clicks his fingers to change the slides.) ... And again... and again... and again... and again...
  The slides change to show a succession of burned and shattered victims. The last one seems charred all over. SIR JAMES watches implacably. BASIL KEYES seems to feel rather sick.
STEIGER (continues): A beermugful of Honey can create a lethal zone for all terrestrial life within an area of 15 acres. Low flying aircraft spraying PL.45 can cover 100 square miles in two hours. This is all I need to finish the job. Thank you.
  The slides finish. The lights come on.
SIR JAMES: Mmm. Impressive. Am I to understand Colonel Steiger, that granted supplies of adequate quantities of .. er ... Honey ... you are prepared to guarantee the internal stability of your territory?
STEIGER: You have my word.
SIR JAMES (standing up, passing his briefcase to MICK): Basil ... a moment ...

SIR JAMES and BASIL KEYES move off towards the projection screen, to talk in confidence. STEIGER joins DR MUNDA as MADAME PAILLARD detaches herself from the group to join MICK. A waiter starts to carry round a silver tray with champagne glasses.

MADAME PAILLARD : Champagne . . Monsieur?
MICK : Thank you very much, Ma'am.

MICK takes a glass. OSWALD, who has been helping himself at the bar, comes up to MICK.

OSWALD : Glad to see you made it, old boy. Stick with the old man. You're on a good wicket. Cheers!
MICK : Cheers!

SIR JAMES and BASIL KEYES are conferring quietly by the screen. They seem to have reached a conclusion.

BASIL KEYES : Yes.
SIR JAMES : Yes.

He clicks his fingers at MICK, who leaves MADAME PAILLARD and OSWALD and comes up to SIR JAMES and BASIL.

MICK (quietly to the others) : Excuse me, excuse me.
SIR JAMES : I don't think you've met my new assistant, Travis. Travis, this is Basil Keyes. I could send Travis along sometime tomorrow.
BASIL KEYES : Well, we've got a night sitting . . . but it should finish before lunch . . . so anywhere near the House of Commons.
SIR JAMES : Right.

SIR JAMES leads the way back to the group standing round DR MUNDA. MICK follows. BASIL KEYES goes to the bar and helps himself to a drink.

SIR JAMES : Mr President. I'll take these documents home with me, if I may. Study them thoroughly. I shan't keep you waiting.

He passes the documents to MICK. A waiter hands them champagne on a tray.

SIR JAMES (clinking glasses with DR MUNDA) : It must be all of 40 years.
DR MUNDA : 39.
SIR JAMES (to MRS NAIDU) : I shared digs with the President's brother.
MRS NAIDU : How nice.
DR MUNDA : I shall never forget that wonderful spring morning in your room in Balliol. You and Peter drunk on the bookshelves . . . Karl Marx and Keynes on the floor.

KEYES joins SIR JAMES and DR MUNDA.
SIR JAMES : How is Peter?
DR MUNDA : In detention alas . . . I was urged to hang him, but for once I was weak. (They all chuckle.)
    The camera moves left to see MICK drinking with OSWALD and MADAME PAILLARD.
BASIL KEYES : Power creates the man. Tacitus. Cheers!
DR MUNDA : Cheers!
    General laughter. MICK drinks his champagne, very pleased with himself.
BLACKOUT

SIR JAMES' HOUSE
    SIR JAMES' Rolls draws up outside a grand, neo classical house.

THE HALL
    MICK follows SIR JAMES into the spacious hall. It is rich and rather sombre, decorated with Jacobean furniture and a catholic selection of paintings. A distinguished butler, JENKINS, takes SIR JAMES' hat. MICK hovers as SIR JAMES goes upstairs.
MICK : Well . . . Goodnight Sir James.
SIR JAMES : Where are you going?
MICK (innocently) : Home, sir.
SIR JAMES : No, no, no—that won't work at all. (To the butler): Jenkins, better show Mr Travis to William's apartment. Get him anything he wants.
    SIR JAMES continues up the marble stairs, followed by JENKINS and MICK. At the top SIR JAMES holds out his hand for his briefcase. MICK gives it to him.
SIR JAMES : Thank you. (To JENKINS) : My wife back yet?
JENKINS : Still at the opera, sir.
SIR JAMES : Ah. . .
    SIR JAMES walks up another staircase towards his bedroom. JENKINS leads MICK in the opposite direction. They go up the stairs and down a corridor.

WILLIAM'S SUITE
    JENKINS comes in the room. He turns on the lights. MICK follows him in. The living room is modern, angular and expensively cool. There is a highly polished oak floor with fur rugs on it. A glass table with coloured stone birds' eggs and 3

telephones on it; a pair of Byzantine icons hang on the walls; large table lamps.

JENKINS (switching on the lamps): This is the living room. Your bedroom is through here. I'll fetch you some pyjamas. Dinner is prawn cocktail and leg of mutton. What would you care to drink?

MICK (testing his new status): Champagne?

JENKINS (with a sniff): Very good, sir.

As JENKINS leaves the living room MICK looks around, very satisfied. There is a hi-fi set on a stand, underneath it a cassette recorder. MICK picks up a tape cassette—puts it on—very loud stereo music cuts in—ALAN'S voice singing. MICK hurriedly turns down the volume. He starts to explore.

ALAN (singing): *Give ... give ... give ... give*
Everything you're paid for
Run ... run ... run ... run
For everything you've prayed for
Keep that smile on your face
With a smile you're welcome any place—
Because the next one will be, the next one will be
The next one will be the best one of the year.

In the bedroom MICK opens a large mahogany wardrobe and finds it empty except for a pair of brightly polished hunting boots in wooden trees. He takes one of the boots and measures it against the sole of his own foot. On top of the wardrobe is a white polo hat and polo sticks. MICK reaches up, takes the hat and puts it on. Two telephones are on the table next to the bed. MICK sits on the bed, takes out PATRICIA'S address book, lifts one of the telephones and dials. The music continues.

MICK (feet up on the bed): Hello, can I speak to Patricia, please... Patricia Burgess... Well, what time do you expect her?... Well, listen, I'm the bloke you picked up last night ... the one in the gold suit... Yes... Actually, I'm personal assistant to her father now... Well, why should I be joking? Listen, can you please get a message to her. (He sits up on the edge of the bed.) It's very important... Yes... Can you please tell her, just tell her I've tamed the Tiger... Yes, yes... Okay... Thank you, thank you.

A buzzer sounds from the living room.

MICK (continuing): She'll understand.... Yes...

MICK quickly puts the phone down and runs into the living room to pick up the first telephone on the glass table.

MICK: Michael Travis speaking...

The buzzer continues. MICK puts down the first phone and lifts the second.
MICK : Michael Travis speaking. . .
The buzzer continues. MICK puts down the second phone and lifts the third.
MICK : Michael Travis speaking. . .
At this moment JENKINS wheels in a trolley. The buzzer continues.
JENKINS : On the wall, sir.
As MICK picks up the internal house phone from the wall, ALAN's voice breaks in from the tape deck. MICK hurriedly turns it off.
MICK : Michael Travis speaking. . . Yes—certainly, Sir James . . . this instant, Sir James.
MICK puts down the phone. JENKINS hands him a glass of champagne.
JENKINS : A sip of champagne first, sir?
MICK takes the glass and starts to drink.
MICK : Thank you, Jenkins. Is Miss Patricia expected this evening, Jenkins?
JENKINS : I've no idea, sir. Miss Patricia is a law unto herself.
MICK hands JENKINS his glass, grabs a prawn from the cocktail glass and turns to leave.
JENKINS : Straight down the corridor. Up the steps. Door facing you at the top.
MICK : Thank you, Jenkins.
JENKINS clears his throat loudly. MICK stops. JENKINS indicates the polo hat. MICK takes it off and leaves. JENKINS fastidiously puts the hat on top of a cupboard.

CORRIDOR

MICK runs down the corridor and up the steps. He stops outside the door, tidies himself and knocks.

SIR JAMES' BEDROOM

SIR JAMES, in pyjamas, sits up in bed with a bedtable across it. He finishes checking a wad of brand new ten pound notes, and inserts them into an envelope.
SIR JAMES : Enter.
MICK enters and waits while SIR JAMES licks the envelope. The room is cosily and comfortably furnished : a well-worn sofa,

an easy chair, some paintings of SIR JAMES' children on the
walls—PATRICIA and a younger child.
SIR JAMES: You remember Keyes? You met him this evening.
MICK: Basil Keyes?
SIR JAMES: The Right Honorable. Go to his club—the National
Political at 2.05 p.m. Tomorrow. Give him . . . this . . .
He picks up the envelope and places it in a copy of *Country
Life*. He gives it to MICK.
SIR JAMES: He'll give you a letter. Here, you'll need a map—
SIR JAMES takes an Ordnance Survey map.
SIR JAMES: You can do a map reference, can you?
MICK (nods): Yes, sir.
SIR JAMES (studying the map): 973 670, church with spire, 3
o'clock, small country lane, first gate on the right. (He gives MICK
the map). That's your rendezvous. Warner will drive you down. I'd
like you back here by seven. What's map reference? Mmm?
MICK: 973 670, sir.
SIR JAMES: Correct.
LADY BURGESS enters from the bathroom in a pink dressing
gown. She carries a tray with two mugs of cocoa.

SIR JAMES: Meet my wife. Mummy this is Michael.
LADY BURGESS: I hope you don't find your mattress too hard. William always liked a hard mattress.
MICK: Thank you very much, Lady Burgess. Everything's perfect.
SIR JAMES (bored with this conversation): Night. . .
MICK: Goodnight, sir.

> MICK turns and makes for the door. LADY BURGESS starts to climb into bed with SIR JAMES. SIR JAMES calls out, sharply.

SIR JAMES: . . . and hold that damn magazine folded—in two—so that the envelope doesn't fall out.

> MICK folds the magazine, running his fingers down the middle, and leaves. LADY BURGESS gives SIR JAMES his bottle of pills. He takes a couple. They sip their cocoa.

LOWER REGENT STREET
SIR JAMES' Rolls Royce drives down Lower Regent Street. Big Ben is striking two o'clock. The car turns and stops by a colonnaded building. WARNER gets out and walks round the car. He opens the door and MICK steps out. He is wearing an impeccable dark suit and a bowler hat.

MICK: Thank you, Warner. . . . About half an hour.

THE NATIONAL POLITICAL CLUB LIBRARY

A GENERAL and a BISHOP stroll away from a coffee table, chatting together. They reveal MICK sitting in a comfortable leather armchair, looking around. He looks up as BASIL KEYES approaches.

BISHOP: I expect your wife misses her horses.
GENERAL: My dear fellow, she never gets out of bed.
BISHOP: Oh, rotten luck.

BASIL KEYES comes up to MICK. MICK rises to shake his hand. They both sit. BASIL KEYES puts a folded copy of *Field* on the table; MICK puts his copy of *Country Life* next to it. A waiter appears.

BASIL: Hello Frank.
WAITER: Good afternoon, sir.
BASIL: Mr Travis will have a . . . ?
MICK: A dry martini. Very dry.
BASIL: A dry martini. Thank you, Frank, and a large Scotch.
WAITER: Thank you, sir.

BASIL KEYES picks up *Country Life*. He flips through it to check that the envelope is there. He takes it out, putting it in his inside breast pocket. MICK picks up *Field* and discreetly fingers through it. He sees a slim beige envelope, which he puts in his inside breast pocket.
BASIL : I don't think you'll run into any trouble. They've got their briefing. They're all good chaps.
MICK : Everything's under control.
FRANK reappears and sets down the two drinks. BASIL and MICK raise their glasses.
BASIL : Good luck... And don't leave any finger prints.
MICK is stabbed by sudden anxiety. BASIL laughs. MICK recovers his cool and laughs with him.
BLACKOUT

LONDON STREET
SIR JAMES' Rolls drives smoothly up St. James'. Luxurious music accompanies it.

ROLLS ROYCE
MICK, seated in the back of the Rolls, carefully peels open the beige envelope. It is marked in heavy black print: 'MINISTRY OF DEFENCE A.1. SECURITY'. MICK opens it and takes out an official form. He studies it. WARNER watches him. The music reaches a point of suspension.

LIMBO
ALAN is at the piano in shirt sleeves. He starts the intro to a number. TOLLY smacks a tambourine. DAVE and COLIN take up the intro as the camera pans onto ALAN. He sings.
ALAN (singing) :
> *When there's a bluebird singing by your window pane*
> *And the sun shines bright all day through—*
> *Don't forget, boy—look over your shoulder*
> *'Cos there's always someone coming after you....*

MOTORWAY
The camera shoots over the bonnet of the Rolls as it speeds down the motorway. It passes under an overhead blue sign: 'A 40 (M) THE WEST (GUILDFORD 30) OXFORD 51'.

ROLLS ROYCE
MICK, riding high in the back of the Rolls, looks about him. He sees a button on a high panel and presses it. The cocktail cabinet opens.
MICK: Like a brandy, Warner?
WARNER: Not for me, sir. I never touch a drop on the job.
MICK: Of course... of course.
MICK leans forward to take out the decanter and a glass. WARNER watches him in the mirror as MICK fills the glass a quarter full. ALAN's voice returns.
ALAN (singing): *When everything in life seems just as it should be,*
At last success seems just around the door—

A COUNTRY ROAD
The Rolls drives on through the sunlit, lyrical afternoon. Trees fringe the road.
ALAN (singing): *Don't forget boy—look over your shoulder*
'Cos things don't stay the same for evermore.

ROLLS ROYCE
MICK makes himself comfortable, lights a cigarette, and watches his reflection in the window. He smooths his hair complacently.
ALAN (singing): *Hope springs eternal in a young man's breast,*
And he dreams of a better life ahead—

LIMBO
ALAN (singing): *Without that dream you are nothing, nothing,*
nothing...
You'll have to find out for yourself that dream is
dead...
dead.... dead.... dead.... dead....

A COUNTRY LANE
As the last word echoes, the Rolls turns off the country road into a secluded lane. It draws to a halt between tall hedgerows and blowing grass. MICK steps out confidently and marches through a gap in the hedge, leaving WARNER by the Rolls.

AERODROME
MICK appears through a gate bearing a notice: 'R.A.F.

KEEP OUT'. He looks round and sees activity on a dispersal area nearby. A large transport aircraft with RAF roundels is being loaded from three RAF ten ton lorries. Drums are being lifted from the lorries by fork-lift trucks. The tin drums are mustard yellow, about three feet high, with skull and crossbones painted on them. They are inscribed PL.45. In the background an RAF FLIGHT SERGEANT supervises the operation. A GROUP CAPTAIN is pacing by an RAF Morris 1100, hands behind his back, occasionally glancing at his watch. Suddenly he sees MICK and comes forward, waving a hand. MICK waves back with his brolley. He closes the gate behind him; they meet and shake hands.

GROUP CAPTAIN: Oh, there you are.
MICK: How do you do. Pleased to meet you. Travis.
CAPTAIN: Wallace. . . Had a good run down?
MICK: Fine, thank you. Fine.
    They walk towards the aircraft.
GROUP CAPTAIN: Got the, er . . . bumph, have you? (MICK gives him the security envelope.) Good, oh. We're nearly there. (He opens the envelope and reads. . .): Good. . . Good . . . good, good, good, good. We're over here.
    They go over towards the FLIGHT SERGEANT.
GROUP CAPTAIN: Sergeant Beevers!
    The FLIGHT SERGEANT comes towards them.
GROUP CAPTAIN: We've got the OK to take off. Do the necessary, will you.
FLIGHT SERGEANT: Yes, sir.
    The GROUP CAPTAIN hands the papers to the FLIGHT SERGEANT, who scans them and then gets out a small transmitter from his jacket. MICK watches the activity with satisfaction.
FLIGHT SERGEANT: Ground Control to pilot-navigator Happy Hippo 5. Destination Honey—Flight AT060—is Zingara International Airport. Take off 15 minutes.
PILOT (voice over): Wilco. Over and out.
    A further load of drums is lifted into the aircraft. The FLIGHT SERGEANT produces a receipt pad with a carbon under the top leaf. He gives it to MICK with a ball point.
FLIGHT SERGEANT: Sign by the cross, sir.
MICK: Oh, thank you.
GROUP CAPTAIN: 12,000 gallons of the stuff there. You could do

half East Africa with that, Mr Travis—(MICK laughs.)
    The FLIGHT SERGEANT gives the top copy back to MICK who puts it in his pocket. MICK and the GROUP CAPTAIN walk away. The FLIGHT SERGEANT stares after them as loading continues.

SIR JAMES' DINING ROOM
An elegant, formal dining room. On the table—a huge bowl of grapes, some fruit and cheese. The guests are seated as follows:

	SIR JAMES	
	DR MUNDA	MADAME PAILLARD
	MRS NAIDU	TIMOTHY SOUZA
	MICK	BASIL KEYES

    JENKINS is patrolling with the coffee pot.
DR MUNDA (selecting a grape from the bowl): And, of course, it was your flag that went up and ours that came down; and the extraordinary thing was that the Duchess never even noticed! (Delighted laughter.)
SIR JAMES: That will be all, thank you, Jenkins. (JENKINS leaves.)

Well, gentlemen . . . to business.
> TIMOTHY SOUZA produces his document case and puts it on the table. He opens it and takes out some documents which he passes across to MRS NAIDU. She checks them and passes them on to DR MUNDA who retains one and passes the other on to SIR JAMES.

TIMOTHY SOUZA: Sir James, we would like the first instalment. . .
DR MUNDA (decisively): . . . in cash.
> SIR JAMES, impassive, calls MICK, who removes his large cigar from his mouth and comes round the table. SIR JAMES takes out pencil and paper and writes down a number.

SIR JAMES: Travis. Here's the combination to the safe in my study. . . . You'll find a case there. Bring it here.
MICK: Yes, sir.
> MICK takes the card and leaves.

HALL
> MICK walks jauntily down the hall towards SIR JAMES' study, cigar in mouth, hands clasped behind his back. He pushes open the door.

SIR JAMES' STUDY
> MICK enters the study. It is like a library: lots of bookshelves half-filled with 'complete works'. A screen divides the room. The safe is in the corner between the bookshelves and the window. MICK holds the piece of paper in one hand and starts to work the dial of the safe with the other. He opens the safe door and takes out a brown leather case. He inspects the contents. As he does so, he hears voices and the sound of a girl's laugh.

MAN (off-screen): Please, darling, please.
GIRL (off-screen): Dickie. . .
> MICK looks up, surprised. The voices are coming from the other side of the screen.

DICKIE: But you must—
GIRL (off-screen): Oh, don't go on, Dickie.
DICKIE: I . . . I've never been very sure of myself. Not until I found you.
GIRL: You drink too much.
DICKIE: I know, you're my last chance.
> MICK moves along the study wall, holding the case. He sees a

man in evening dress kneeling before a girl who is sprawled across a chair. It is PATRICIA, seductively dressed in a low-cut white gown, her hair in a chignon. She is wearing diamond earrings, necklace and bracelet, and a white fur stole. The man turns and sees MICK.

DICKIE: My God!
    He stands in confusion, rearranges his clothing and dashes from the room.
PATRICIA: Michael!
    MICK comes over to her.
MICK: Patricia! What are you doing here?
PATRICIA (teasing): This is my home.
MICK: Well, who was that?
PATRICIA: Dickie—the Duke of Belminster—he's an old friend of mine.
MICK: What does he want?
PATRICIA: He wants to marry me.
    She goes over to the mantelpiece, provocatively, and picks up a bottle of champagne. She pours out a glass.
MICK: Well, you can't.

She giggles.
PATRICIA: I might. I haven't decided yet...
MICK: But I love you and I'm going to marry you...
He hoists the case onto a table and displays the contents.
MICK: Look!
PATRICIA (laughing at him): Oh, Michael. You're so hopelessly conventional.
She comes closer and very deliberately kisses him, hard.
MICK (slightly shattered): I told you I was going to be a success, and I am.
He shuts the case and picks it up.
PATRICIA: I did warn you.
MICK: Wait here for me.
He gives her a quick kiss and leaves with the case. She looks after him, then crosses to the mantelpiece, puts down her glass and looks up at the gold-framed picture hanging on the wall. It is a Renoir. Speedily, but deliberately she opens her white evening bag and extracts a small, pearl handled penknife. She opens the knife, pulls a chair to the fireplace, and proceeds to cut the Renoir out of its frame.

SIR JAMES' DINING ROOM
    MICK enters and places the heavy case on the table. DR MUNDA and SIR JAMES are completing the signing of the documents.
SIR JAMES : Thank you, Michael.
MRS NAIDU : Sir James, we need a witness.
SIR JAMES : Travis!
    He hands his pen to MICK, who goes over to add his signature. SIR JAMES invites DR MUNDA and TIMOTHY SOUZA to inspect the contents of the case. SOUZA opens the case while SIR JAMES retreats to the fireplace. MICK watches as DR MUNDA runs his hands over the gleaming gold bars. Suddenly a telephone buzzes. Everyone looks round. SIR JAMES answers.
SIR JAMES (discomposed): Who? . . . I see . . . Yes—of course not. Show them up. . . (He turns to the group at the table) : The Fraud Squad. (They all rise with varying degrees of alarm.) : Now please, everyone, keep quite calm. Inspector Carding is a very decent fellow. Mr Souza—if you please. . .
    TIMOTHY SOUZA closes the case.
SIR JAMES : Travis.
    He indicates the signed documents to MICK, who brings them over.
SIR JAMES (to MICK): Put those in your pocket. (To TIMOTHY SOUZA) : The case please. . . Sit down. (Giving the case to MICK) : Hold this.
    SOUZA goes to his seat. MICK is left standing, a sacrificial lamb. The door opens and INSPECTOR CARDING is ushered in by JENKINS. Two plain-clothed policemen in light macintoshes follow.
JENKINS : Inspector Carding.
SIR JAMES : Good evening, Inspector.
CARDING : Good evening, Sir James. . . . I'm sorry to disturb you, Sir James.
SIR JAMES : Not at all. I think you know everybody here. (MRS NAIDU puts on her glasses.) Except, perhaps, my new assistant—Michael Travis. He—hasn't been with me very long.
    There is a peculiar weight to SIR JAMES' last words. It does not escape INSPECTOR CARDING.
CARDING : It is Mr Travis I wish to interview, with your permission, of course.
    CARDING nods to one of the policemen. He opens the door and in marches the FLIGHT SERGEANT from the Honey loading.

CARDING : Now, is there anyone here you recognise?
FLIGHT SERGEANT : Yes. (He raises his arm and points accusingly at MICK): That is the man.
CARDING : Thank you, Beevers. (The FLIGHT SERGEANT salutes, and marches out.) I beg your pardon, Mr Travis, may I have that bag?
MICK looks for assurance from SIR JAMES, who nods. CARDING takes the case from MICK.
CARDING : Just a minute...
Both policemen come over and search MICK. One finds the document, and the other finds the RAF docket. They give them to CARDING, who holds up the Zingaran document against the light.
CARDING (to MICK): Did you sign this, sir?
MICK : Yes.
The guests innocently smoke their cigarettes and cigars as CARDING examines the document.
CARDING (to MICK) : Is this your signature, sir?
MICK again looks to SIR JAMES, who again nods with intimate reassurance.
MICK : Er ... yes.
CARDING (to DR MUNDA): Is this your signature, sir?
DR MUNDA (with heavy certainty): No.
CARDING (to SIR JAMES): Is this your signature, sir?
SIR JAMES (taking the document): Oh, no. . . . Complete forgery. Not worth the paper it's written on.
CARDING (to policeman): Bag, please.
He opens the case. He looks at MICK.
CARDING : Do you realise, sir, it's an offence to export bullion from the United Kingdom without the permission of the Bank of England?
MICK : Yes...
CARDING : When I came into this room, that bag was in your possession?
MICK (looking at SIR JAMES): Yes.
CARDING (indicating departure): Would you mind, sir.
MICK turns to SIR JAMES in sudden alarm. SIR JAMES looks meaningful.
SIR JAMES : All right, Michael, trust me.
MICK, reassured, is escorted from the room by the two policemen.
SIR JAMES : I'll take that, Carding.

He stretches out his hand for the case. CARDING gives him a look of amused, respectful complicity. Playing the game.
CARDING: I'm so sorry to have disturbed you, Sir James... Dr Munda.

He leaves and closes the door.

SIR JAMES sits down at the table again. The atmosphere relaxes.

SIR JAMES: The dividing line between the House of Lords and Pentonville Gaol is very, very thin.

Everybody laughs.

SIR JAMES' ENTRANCE HALL

MICK is marched between the two policemen down the hall following CARDING. Suddenly they stop. MICK stops too. One of the policemen suddenly grabs MICK, the other punches him viciously in the stomach and face. The first policeman rabbit-punches him expertly and takes off his macintosh. He throws it over MICK's head. CARDING watches. They drag him out.

THE REHEARSAL ROOM

ALAN PRICE is at the piano, now wearing a black anorak and white shirt. He removes a cigar from his mouth and starts to sing, amused. The camera moves in.

ALAN (singing): *We all want justice,*
> *But you got to have money to buy it*
> *You'd have to be a fool to close your eyes and deny it*
> *There's a lot of poor people who are walking the streets of my town*
> *Too blind to see that justice is used to do them right down.*
>
> *All through life from beginning to end you pay your monthly instalments*
> *Next to health is wealth and only wealth will buy you justice*
> *Money... Justice... Money... Justice... Money ...Justice*

OLD BAILEY

The last words of the song are heard as the image changes to

the Royal Coat of Arms above the JUDGE's bench. The camera moves down to discover the JUDGE in full oratorical flight.

MICK is standing in the dock between two policemen. His face is bruised and he has two black eyes. The camera tilts up over the Court to show the JUDGE again. The music gives way to his words.

JUDGE : . . . As we go through this weary vale of tears the more valuable it becomes—our deposit account of innocence. Now, Travis was given a position of great trust by his benefactor, one of England's most eminent industrialists. He repaid that trust by seeking to export for his own gain £10,000,000 of his employer's money. (Bewigged functionaries look at MICK.) Was this the action of an innocent? (The jury of respectable citizens look severely at MICK's bruised face.) If such perfidy can be committed without fear of retribution, then how can the rule of law, patriotism, duty, the very basis of our society hope to survive? Well, go and consider your verdict carefully... And take your time...

The JUDGE rises and the LADY USHER stands.

LADY USHER : Be upstanding in Court.

Everyone in the Court stands. The JUDGE bows to the jury and bows to the Court. The LADY USHER opens the door for the JUDGE.

JUDGE'S CHAMBERS

The JUDGE enters his chambers after the LADY USHER. Law books line the shelves. The LADY USHER comes up behind the JUDGE to remove his gown. He unhooks his robes and she removes his entire costume. He is left naked except for his wig and a pair of scarlet bikini briefs. The LADY USHER hangs up his clothes and crosses the room to open a small cupboard in the oak panelling. It contains a variety of whips and birches. The JUDGE points and selects a small cat o' nine tails, then moves to a long polished table. He lies down on it, arms outstretched, looking forward like an expectant sphinx. The LADY USHER comes to the table. She starts to lash him.

BLACKOUT

OLD BAILEY

The Court is re-assembled.

The LADY USHER enters and bangs twice with her rod. All stand.

FEMALE USHER : Be upstanding in Court.
    The JUDGE enters, once again fully robed. He sits. Everyone sits.
JUDGE (addressing the jury) : Members of the jury, have you arrived at a verdict on which you are all agreed.
CHIEF OF JURY : We have, my Lord.
    MICK glances apprehensively.
JUDGE : Do you find the prisoner guilty, or not guilty?
CHIEF OF JURY : Guilty, my Lord.
JUDGE : May I say how entirely I agree with that verdict.
FEMALE USHER : The prisoner will stand to receive sentence.
    MICK stands.
JUDGE (with all the dignity of established truth) : Society is based on good faith, on a commonly accepted bond. It is the inflamed greed of people like you, Michael Travis, that has led to the present breakdown of our society. (MICK stands listening.) Before I pass sentence, have *you* anything to say?
MICK (with all his heart) : My Lord—I did my duty. I only wanted to be successful. I did my best.
JUDGE (the knell of doom) : And you failed...

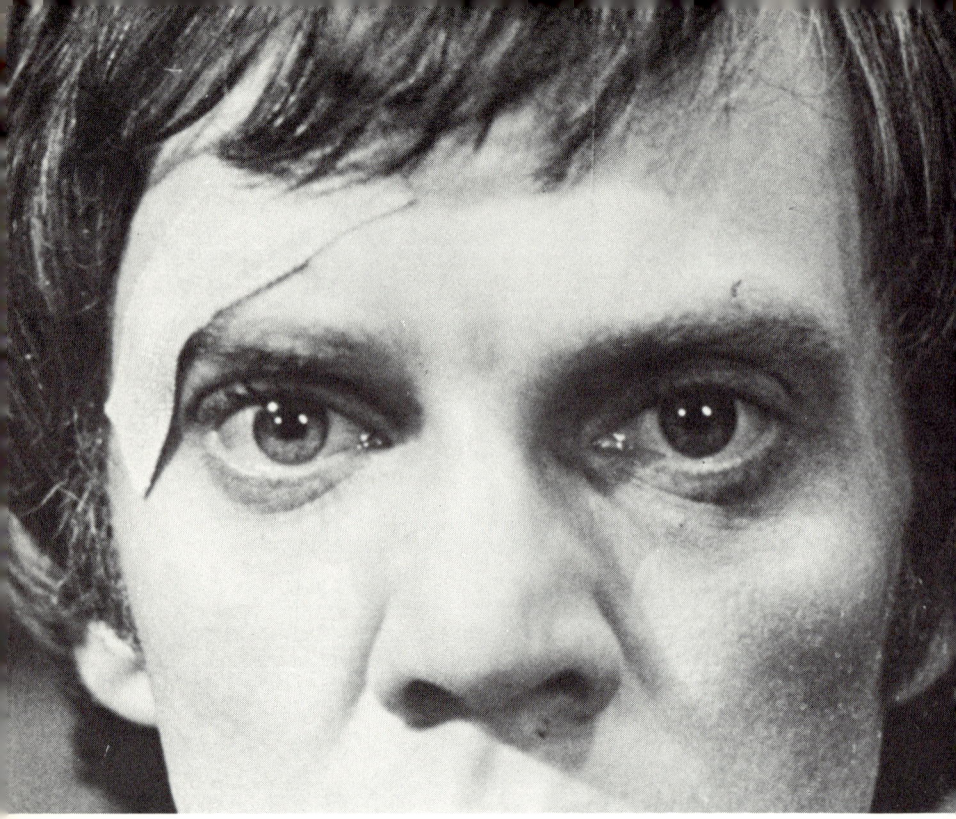

MICK: I am innocent, my Lord.
JUDGE (his eyes flash): I sentence you to five years hard labour.
   BLACKOUT

   Close-up of MICK's desperate eyes.
TITLE: *GUILTY!*
   The jury and barristers stare accusingly at MICK.
TITLE: *FIVE YEARS!*
   The JUDGE...
TITLE: *THERE ARE 3,750 MILLION HUMAN BEINGS ALIVE ON OUR WORLD TODAY. 17 MILLION OF THEM ARE IN PRISON.*

   PRISON FACADE
   The prison is massive, like a fortress.
TITLE: *LEARNING TO LIVE A GOOD AND USEFUL LIFE*

Pigeons descend and settle on the prison roof.

TITLE : *BEHIND BARS* . . .

The prison façade again.

TITLE : *STONE WALLS* . . .

The caged windows of the prison.

TITLE : *BECOMING BETTER*

The prisoners wave through the bars.

TITLE : *AND SO WITH MICHAEL.*

WITH UNDERSTANDING AND
COMPASSION AND A LAVISH
EXPENDITURE OF PUBLIC MONEY
THE PRISON AUTHORITIES
DEVOTE THEMSELVES TO MAKING
A NEW MAN OF HIM.
FOR FIVE YEARS . . .
AND THEY SUCCEED

BLACKOUT

MICK'S CELL
The wall of MICK's cell. Every day of every week of his five-year sentence is marked on it in coloured chalk. In front of the wall, MICK is sitting on his bed, tending a dove and murmuring to it gently.
MICK : I won't hurt. Don't be frightened. Be gentle, be gentle. . . Let's have a look at you. That's better.
  MICK unties a splint from the bird's leg and unwraps a bandage. He takes the bird to the window to release it through the bars.
  An eye appears at the peep-hole in his cell door : as it watches MICK's goodness, it crinkles in benign approval.
  MICK watches the bird fly away into the sky.
  Followed by the eye, MICK goes to his small, make-shift desk. A text on the wall above the desk reads : 'HE PRAYETH BEST, WHO LOVETH BEST ALL THINGS BOTH GREAT AND SMALL'. On the desk are a large diary, several ball-points, felt-tipped pens and a row of books—*The Lower*

Depths by Maxim Gorky and Bertrand Russell's *History of Western Philosophy*. There are pictures on the wall by MICK's bed—Dr Schweitzer, Maxim Gorky, Bertrand Russell. He takes them down and reverently places them in his diary.

The door of the cell is unlocked. A WARDER appears—kindly of voice and visage.

WARDER: All right, Travis, you've done your stretch. Smarten up for the Governor.

MICK rises, takes his jacket and follows the WARDER.

WARDER: Well done, lad.

PRISON GOVERNOR'S OFFICE

MICK stands to attention before the GOVERNOR. The WARDER stands behind MICK. The severity of the office is brightened with vases of flowers from the prison gardens. There is a sofa. The GOVERNOR's large desk is rather like a headmaster's. Portraits and long group photographs cover the walls. The GOVERNOR, middle-aged, moustached, well-meaning, is standing behind his desk.

GOVERNOR: Well, Travis, you're free. Free to rejoin the world of decent, ordinary men and women who are content to earn their daily bread by the sweat of their brow. The brotherhood of man, Travis.

MICK'S look is pure and simple to the point of idiocy. He has been purged of his brash ambition.

MICK: I know where I went wrong, sir. I've been thinking...

GOVERNOR: Good lad.

MICK: I've read books, and I see things differently now, sir.

The GOVERNOR rises and walks round the desk to confront MICK.

GOVERNOR: Well, now, tell me, have you er . . . have you any plans?

MICK: No plans, sir. I just want to get out there and learn to be a proper human being, sir.

The GOVERNOR looks at MICK, shrewdly as he imagines...

GOVERNOR: I'd like to . . . I'd like to read you something. I think it may help.

He picks up a small, ancient book from the desk and reads.

GOVERNOR: 'One that never turned his back
But marched breast forward...
Never doubted clouds would break...
Never dreamed that wrong would triumph...;
Held we fall to rise . . . sleep to wake.'

The camera has tracked in to MICK, responding to these inspiring words. The GOVERNOR closes the book and takes off his glasses.

GOVERNOR: I'd like you to have this. It belonged to my grandmother, but you may find it will help you through the difficult days that lie ahead....

He gives the book to MICK.

MICK: Thank you very much, sir.

The GOVERNOR is moved.

GOVERNOR: Oh, I've sensed that spark of idealism in you, and that can move mountains. You know that. (He looks intently into MICK'S eyes.) For a man like you, Travis . . . Michael . . . for a boy like you. . . you're still young, everything is possible. The world is your oyster. . . . I can see you stripped, building motorways. (MICK responds to the vision like Joan of Arc. The GOVERNOR pauses, then . . .): You have eyes like Steve McQueen, did anyone ever tell you that?

He kisses MICK on the forehead. MICK looks at the GOVERNOR.

The WARDER is still standing to attention, having watched the whole scene impassively.
GOVERNOR: Goodbye Travis . . . and good luck!

THE GAOL GATE
A small door in the high prison gate opens, and the WARDER's voice is heard from within.
WARDER: Macintyre. Biles. Williams. Travis.
Three men, whose faces we probably recognise, step out into freedom. MICK is the last. For a moment, they stand grouped in the courtyard, the prison walls looming behind them.
In the road before them are waiting a pretty girl in slacks by a sports car, and an elderly lady in a fur coat by a Rover.
WILLIAMS turns first, shaking hands all round. He straightens his tie and runs off.
WILLIAMS: Goodbye old chap. I'll send you a postcard.
WILLIAMS embraces the girl. The ELDERLY LADY calls imperiously.
ELDERLY LADY: Lawrence!
BILES breaks from MICK and runs off.
BILES: Mummy!
MACINTYRE shakes hands with MICK, moved.
MACINTYRE: Thank you, Mick, for everything. . .
MICK: Goodbye. Best of luck.
MACINTYRE (warmly): Thank you.
MICK watches MACINTYRE hurry off with his suitcase. WILLIAMS and his girlfriend drive off in the sports car; BILES and his mother get into the Rover.
The WARDER speaks from the doorway; he comes up to MICK.
WARDER: On your own? You on your own, then?
MICK: Yes.
WARDER: Got nowhere to go?
MICK: I'll manage.
WARDER: Just a minute. . .
He turns away to write an address on a piece of paper. The Rover drives up.
BILES: Do you want a lift?
MICK: I'm going the other way.
MICK waves as the car drives off.
WARDER (giving MICK an address): Here.
MICK: What is it?

WARDER: It's in the East End. Give you a start there. Be good.
MICK (smiling): I won't be seeing you anymore.
WARDER: Well, good luck.
> They shake hands. The WARDER steps back over the threshold of the prison. He turns.

WARDER: It may not be as easy as you think.
> MICK looks back at the WARDER, surprised. The door clangs shut.

BLACKOUT

LONDON SKYLINE
> The camera pans down past a large slogan painted on a high wall: 'TAKE COURAGE'. A Salvation Army band is playing a hymn, *How Sweet the Name of Jesus Sounds*, on the corner of a working-class street below. A sparse crowd stands idly around. A large lorry drives past; a workman wheels a barrow. MICK comes across the street and stops to look and listen. A Salvation Army WOMAN, mild and wide-eyed, has been passing a collection box round the crowd. She sees MICK and offers him her box.

WOMAN: Would you like to help?
MICK (cheerfully): Oh. Sure I would.
> MICK pulls out a brown envelope and opens it. The WOMAN eyes him knowingly.

WOMAN: Are you sure you can spare it?
MICK: Gladly.
WOMAN: You're from the prison, aren't you?
MICK: That's right.
WOMAN: There's no need to be ashamed.
> MICK sticks two pounds in the collection box.

MICK (blithely): I'm not ashamed.
WOMAN (seeing the notes): Glory Alleluia! Major, Major!
> She runs across to the Salvation Army MAJOR and speaks low, excited, into his ear. The MAJOR abruptly stops the band from playing. He is middle-aged, authoritative, with thin, wire-framed glasses.

MAJOR: Brothers! Today we have with us a young man who has turned over a completely new leaf! He has only just left prison, yet he has given generously of his meagre store.
> Salvation Army cries of 'Glory Alleluia'.
> Two mean-looking customers turn and look at MICK.

MAJOR: Friend—will you step up beside me and bear witness.
MICK (coming forward, pleasantly): Bear witness? What to?
MAJOR: Your sins.
MICK (earnestly): I don't believe in sin.
> This statement creates shock among the Salvationists.

WOMAN: Everybody sins—we know.
MAJOR: Brother—be warned—you stand in great danger.
MICK: I thought like you, once, sir. But now I've learned better. People are good if you give them the chance.
> The two mean-looking customers push into MICK. He apologises nicely; they excuse themselves.

MICK: Excuse me. Sorry, sorry.
MAN: Sorry, mate.
MICK (in full moral flight): We've got to start with humanity. We must try and trust one another.
> The two men sort through the things they have picked from MICK's pocket: his wallet, his prison wages, a pen, a set of keys and his improving book.

MICK: People are good. Everyone has goodness in them. It's poverty, that's why people commit crimes.
MAJOR (joining battle): It's not poverty, Laddie, it's the old Adam. ... Pride! ... Envy! ... Gluttony! ... Sloth! ...
MICK: A great philosopher once wrote ... (he turns to the crowd): something I'd like you all to hear.
> He puts his hand down to his pocket for the improving book. It's not there. As he begins to search, one of the men slips it quickly into the other pocket. MICK pulls it out.

MICK (reading): 'My country is the world... and my religion is to do good.'—Tom Paine.
MAJOR: Tom Paine denied God!
MICK: He believed in Mankind!
> The MAJOR is deeply shocked at MICK's humanistic heresy.

MAJOR: Brother, we will pray for you. Let us all kneel together, friends...
> They all kneel, including the two thieves and shut their eyes. MICK looks round, listens, and then leaves, the book open in his hand.

MAJOR: Oh Lord, look down in mercy on this our misguided
brother—

> Guide his feet into the way of life—
> Remove the blindfold from his eyes—

Let him see the seeds of corruption that are within him
And the hope of Salvation that lies without—
Lift up his gaze to the eternal hills
From whence cometh our only help.
Amen.
CROWD : Amen.
MICK is looking back as he walks away, his book still open in his hand. There is a sudden clatter of footsteps and two men and an aproned woman dash past out of nowhere. The second man collides with MICK, knocking the book from his hand. MICK picks it up, brushing it carefully.
MAJOR (off-screen) : 'Bringing in the sheaves!'
VOICES SINGING (off-screen) : *Sowing in the morning, sowing seeds*
of kindness,
Sowing in the noontide and the
dewy eve. . .
The men grab a ladder from against a wall and dash back past MICK, urged on by the woman. She leads them round a corner. MICK watches curiously, pockets his book, picks up his carrier-bag and follows them.

TENEMENT COURTYARD

Tall grey buildings loom over a central court. People are clustered at the bottom of the courtyard, looking up at a flat with closed windows. Women are hanging out of windows, and over the railings that mark the open staircase running up the centre of the block. The two men and the woman dash with their ladder down the centre of the courtyard, calling out : 'Mind your backs!' 'Out of the way!'. MICK follows them, takes in the scene and moves forward, inquisitively. The men prop their ladder against the wall. It barely reaches the second floor windows. One of the men starts to climb. The three women at the landing railings mock the man.
1ST WOMAN : You burk. It's too flipping short. (To her neighbour) : Hey, look at him.
2ND WOMAN : What are you trying to do? Pick apples?
1ST WOMAN : Picking apples . . . ha, ha, ha.
MICK looks up towards the laughing women. They call out to him.
1ST WOMAN (yelling down to MICK) : Here, you! You!
MICK looks over his shoulder.

2ND WOMAN: Here you, you down there...
1ST WOMAN: You with the bag.
2ND WOMAN: No, not you.... You! (MICK catches on.) Bring up that bleeding bar. The big one.
> MICK turns and picks out a rusty iron bar from a heap of rubbish behind him ... old motor car engines, axles, tyres.

2ND WOMAN: The big one... That's right ... bring it up here.
1ST WOMAN: Up here...
2ND WOMAN: Come on, mate. Move. Bring it up here.
> MICK runs with the bar up the tenement staircase to the third floor landing.

LANDING
> MICK arrives on the landing, surrounded by chattering women.

1ST WOMAN: Come on up here. Get this door open.
2ND WOMAN: Better be quick.
ANOTHER: Bash it.
> MICK beats against the door with the bar.

2ND WOMAN: Better be quick.
1ST WOMAN: Mrs Richards!

ALL: Mrs Richards! Mrs Richards!
2ND WOMAN: Come out of there!
1ST WOMAN: Come on out.
   MICK gives up. He turns to the women.
2ND WOMAN: She's put the bed against the door and double-bolted it.
1ST WOMAN: She's going to do it this time. You mark my words.
2ND WOMAN: Selfish bitch. She's got the kids in there with her.
1ST WOMAN: She'll probably do them in an' all.
MICK: What's the matter? What's wrong?
1ST WOMAN: What's wrong he says!
   They all laugh.
2ND WOMAN: She's going to kill herself. That's what's wrong.
MICK: Can't you stop her?
1ST WOMAN: Well, go on then. *You* stop her . . . nobody's holding you back, are they?
   MICK turns away from the women.

TENEMENT FACADE
   MICK comes down and peers over the railings, followed by the clucking women. They are three storeys up. He sees MRS RICHARDS' windows, a few feet away. He swings his leg over the rails. The women moan with excitement and cover their eyes. Below, the little crowd stirs. MICK reaches out for a drainpipe, gets a foothold and manages to clamber across to MRS RICHARDS' window sill.

MRS RICHARDS' FLAT
   MICK appears at the window. He peers in, crouching on the sill. He knocks.
MICK: Mrs Richards!
   The room inside is drab and poor, but neat. A little boy is sitting silently on a chair against the wall, his legs dangling. MRS RICHARDS is on her knees in an apron, swabbing the floor. MICK bangs the top half of the window open. He wedges his head in.
MICK: Mrs Richards! What are you doing?
MRS RICHARDS (looking up at him): Cleaning the floor. What's it look like?
MICK (at window): What's all this about killing yourself?
   MRS RICHARDS gets up off her knees and throws the cleaning

rag into the bucket.
MRS RICHARDS : I've had enough.
She starts to dust.
MICK : You've been shut up here too long. Think of the world outside.
MRS RICHARDS turns her back on MICK and continues her compulsive cleaning.
MICK : Mrs Richards, now, please. Stop it. I want you to listen.
MRS RICHARDS (crossing to the mantelpiece) : My husband has to find the place looking nice. I'll not have him saying I did wrong in the end.
MICK : You should meet some people. Make some nice friends!
MRS RICHARDS : I haven't been out since we had Penny. That's six years.
MICK : Take a holiday!
MRS RICHARDS : Harry's off work. He hasn't had a job for four years.
MICK : Well, think of the children. I mean, they're the only ones who matter!
MRS RICHARDS reaches into the corner; she polishes a cheap brass tray.
MRS RICHARDS : How can I keep a child clean? How much do you think a pair of kid's shoes costs? The cheapest? £1.20.
MICK : Life's a gift, Mrs Richards. You haven't the right to throw it away.
MRS RICHARDS replaces the carpet in the centre of the room. She looks up to MICK. She moves the table back onto the carpet as she speaks.
MRS RICHARDS : Look, this is the food I buy each week for ourselves and the kids : 7 loaves of bread
    20 lbs of potatoes
    $\frac{3}{4}$ of a pound of tea
    1 packet of porridge oats
    2 packets of cornflakes
MICK : There's always tomorrow. . .
MRS RICHARDS : 1 packet of Co-op soap powder
    3 or 4 pounds of cabbage
    2 swedes
    Custard powder
    Baked beans sometimes
    Tinned tomatoes sometimes

>   Tinned spaghetti sometimes
>   Lettuce when cheap.

MICK: Food isn't everything. Fresh air! Sunshine!
> He gestures to the great outside, slips and nearly falls. MRS RICHARDS turns away and calls into the other room.

MRS RICHARDS: Penny!

LITTLE GIRL (off-screen): Yes, mum.

MRS RICHARDS: Bring the Brasso.
> PENNY, aged about six, comes in with the brasso.

MRS RICHARDS: Now I want you to go over there, love. Wash the big pan under the hot tap. Get off every bit of tomato soup before your Dad gets back.
> She guides the little girl over to the sink in the corner beneath the window.
> MICK has an inspiration. Hurriedly, he gets out the prison governor's book.

MICK: Mrs Richards! Mrs Richards! Please listen to this, Mrs Richards! Now please listen!
> She looks up at him.

MICK (reading): 'Life is mostly froth and bubble
>   Two things stand like stone,
>   Kindness in another's trouble,
>   Courage in your own.'

MRS RICHARDS (blank): Who said that?

MICK: Adam Lindsay Gordon. He was a poet.

MRS RICHARDS: More of a fool, if you ask me.
> She moves back to the table and starts to take off her apron.

MICK: Oh wait there, Mrs Richards! Now wait, Mrs Richards! Wait Mrs Richards! Listen to this, please, Mrs Richards!
> At the fireplace now, she takes her comb out of her handbag and begins to comb her hair. MICK tries to find the page.

MICK: Mrs Richards!
> She turns to MICK. She has ceased to take any notice of his words.

MRS RICHARDS: Tell Harry to leave a note for the milkman. Two pints. (Calling): Penny!

PENNY: Yes, mum.
> PENNY comes to her mother. MRS RICHARDS kisses her as MICK reads.

MICK: 'There's a special providence in the fall of a sparrow.'
>   —*Hamlet*

MRS RICHARDS (giving PENNY a pat): Now go and sit down, love.
As MRS RICHARDS crosses back to kiss the little boy, quiet all this time, MICK starts again.
MICK: Please listen, Mrs Richards! Please listen to this!
'One that never turned his back,
But marched breast forward . . .
Never doubted clouds would break—'
MRS RICHARDS stares at him for a second, then walks firmly into the other room. MICK shouts after her.
MICK: Every cloud has a silver lining, Mrs Richards! . . . Mrs Richards!
He moves past the window, following her.

TENEMENT FACADE
MICK tries to climb onto the window sill of the adjoining room. He reaches out, grasps a drainpipe, gets a foothold and then leaves the security of his window sill. Gasps from below. Now he is hanging onto the drainpipe between the windows. His book slips from his hand and flutters to the ground. He reaches across to the next window-frame.
MICK: Mrs Richards!
He feels himself slipping: grabs the pipe with both hands. A rusty joint gives way; the pipe breaks from the wall. For a moment MICK hangs in space, then the pipe comes clean away and he falls. Sky, buildings, ground whirl past.
BLACKOUT

THE REHEARSAL ROOM
Hands strike a piano keyboard. The camera tilts up to ALAN's face as he sings. . . *My Home Town*.
ALAN (singing): *Down on the corner of the street*
Where I was born we used to meet
And sing the old songs,
We called them dole songs.
In long shot we see ALAN at his piano, COLIN perched beside him, strumming his banjo.
ALAN (singing): *And we'd harmonise so clear*
Even though it was the beer
That made the tears run
About the years gone by. . . .

THE TENEMENT NIGHT
The song continues over as a Policeman, flashing his torch, walks down the pavement in the empty, dark courtyard.

Alan (singing): *We'd go home and kiss the wife,*
Hoping a kiss could change your life...

THE REHEARSAL ROOM
Alan in close shot again...

Alan (singing): *That's how romance is*
No second chances
Back in my home town.

THE TENEMENT NIGHT
The Policeman comes up to the railings. His torch shines down onto Mick, who lies unconscious in the area. The torchlight sweeps across his face—his eyes flicker open. The piano continues. The Policeman is looking down at Mick.

Title: *WHAT'S GOING ON HERE?*

Mick looks up, bewildered.

Title: *WHERE AM I?*

The Policeman, walking round the railings.

Title: *YOU'RE TRESPASSING...*

Mick scrambles to his feet. He looks up, pale.

Title: *WHAT HAPPENED TO MRS RICHARDS?*

The Policeman, impassive.

Title: *SHE KILLED HERSELF.*

He reaches forward and pulls Mick roughly through the railings. Mick puts his hand in his pocket for his wallet.

Title: *I'VE LOST MY WALLET ... ALL MY MONEY.*

The Policeman walks down the railings, shining his torch. The light falls on Mick's brown paper carrier-bag in a doorway.

Title: *IS THIS YOURS?*

Mick walks to the bag. He nods. The Policeman grabs him roughly by the shoulder.

Title: *NOW PISS OFF!*

 The Policeman shoves Mick off into the dark.
 Mick walks away over the square. Half way across, he stops, turns and looks back at the tenement.

Alan (singing): ...*Things aren't so very different now*
       Poor folk must get along somehow
       You live forever on the never never
       Back in my home town.

 DERELICT AREA
 The camera tilts down out of the night sky to a van, open at the back. A cheerful Lady Social Worker is serving soup from the back of the van to a huddle of derelicts. Mick appears, trudging along with his carrier-bag. Painted on the wall behind him is the slogan: 'REVOLUTION IS THE OPIUM OF THE INTELLECTUALS'.

Lady: No queue jumping. Keep in line. Remember—only one bun each. . . . Evening, Mrs Todd; that's a nice coat you've got. (She pours soup into a plastic cup that Mrs Todd has taken from a

cellophane roll.) You feeling better now, Arthur?
ARTHUR, an elderly man with grey hair, stands by the counter.
ARTHUR: Got black-locks in me bed again.
LADY: Oh, chin up—better than rats. Have some bread and butter.
ARTHUR: Got any jam?
LADY: Yes.
   She reaches up to a shelf and takes down a bowl of jam. MICK emerges out of the darkness as she puts it on the counter.
LADY (to ARTHUR): Tuck in. (Seeing MICK): Hello! A new face—don't be shy. Down on your luck? (Pouring soup for him): Here you get this inside you. . . . Watch out—it's hot.
MICK: Thank you.
LADY: Arthur, you are making a mess.
   ARTHUR is sloppily trying to butter himself a slice of bread. His hands are tied in dirty bandages. MICK has been watching ARTHUR, his cup of hot soup raised to his lips. He puts down the cup, and turns to ARTHUR.
MICK: Here, I'll do that for you.
LADY (as MICK starts to butter the bread): He likes it thick. Oh, super! Thanks awfully! (An elderly woman comes up with some dirty cups and hands them to the LADY.) Oh, good girl, Vera. That's lovely, dear.
   ARTHUR watches very carefully as MICK spreads on the jam. When he finishes, he gives the slice to ARTHUR who shuffles off. MICK turns back to the LADY, licking his fingers.
LADY (referring to ARTHUR): Arthritis. Incurable. Be dead in six months, poor old thing.
MICK: Do you do this every night?
LADY: Whenever I can. Well, I have so much time in the evenings.
MICK: Do you get paid for it?
LADY: Good lord, no! One has to do what one can to help.
MICK (his humanism burns still): Can I help?
LADY: That's extremely kind—I can use all the help I can get. Here. You grab hold of this. (She passes MICK a large soup tureen.) Any more cups, please. . . (To MICK): Won't be a jiff. (She turns and goes back into the van.)
   Still holding the tureen, MICK takes the empty soup cups that the old men and women pass to him. He puts them on the counter. The LADY comes round to the back of the van where MICK and the old people are finishing the clearing up. She locks the back doors.

LADY (to the derelicts): Thank you. Good night.
MICK (to the derelicts): Good night.
LADY: See you tomorrow. (To MICK): They do so appreciate it. Even I need sleep, of course. Get's a bit of a grind on one's own. Even the strongest stumble . . . Still, one does what one can. . .

  MICK and the LADY walk round to the front of the vehicle. She is carrying a tube of paper cups wrapped in cellophane.

LADY (looking into the darkness): Now, you see that bonfire over there?

  MICK looks at flickering fires in the distant dark. Indistinct shapes huddle in the firelight and in the shadows. The LADY hands him the roll of paper cups.

LADY: That's all my regulars. Now, you just toddle across and give them their soup. . . . You'll find some of them a bit touchy, but they're all real characters.

  She slides open the van door and gets into the driver's seat.
  MICK gets anxious.

MICK: Yes, but what shall I say? What shall I do?
LADY (breezily): Oh, it's simple. Just be yourself. Don't put on an act. They don't like that. (She starts the motor.)

MICK: Oh, where are you going?
LADY (shouting): I've got the railway stations to do. Oh—leave the impedimenta at the side of the road. . . . Be back about five. Byeeeee! . . .
    The van reverses with a roar.
MICK: Bye!
    The van drives off and MICK is left alone among blowing papers. He looks over at the bonfires. A murmur of voices.

BOMB SITE
    The fires have been lit in the centre of the site. Ruined walls loom around. Beds, old mattresses, doors, etc, burn. Some of the meths drinkers huddle as close as possible to the fires, others shelter against oil drums or walls. The camera moves across two old women sleeping near the fires, then onto three old men. MICK picks his way over the site, past heaps of rubble, carrying his soup and the cups. He bends down.
MICK: Hot soup?
    A bundled-up woman sits up. MICK puts down his carrier-bag and takes one of the cups from the cellophane wrapping. He ladles the soup into her cup. A long-faced tramp turns and stares at MICK. A dishevelled girl cradles a man in grubby evening dress. She looks across at MICK. Is this PATRICIA?
    MICK moves on to another tramp nearer the fire. A woman stares after him, sad-eyed. MICK ladles soup into the tramp's cup. The tramp drinks . . . and spits it out.
TRAMP: Cat's piss. . . Ugh. . . (MICK walks on): Eh, d'ye have any pepper? . . . Pepper? . . .
    MICK steps across a row of sleeping tramps; one, haggard and wild-eyed, stares fixedly after him. He comes up to an elderly couple dressed in rags. The woman's face is bloated by alcohol; she is laughing to herself. The man is swigging purple liquid from an old Johnnie Walker bottle.
MICK: Hot soup, sir?
TRAMP (slurred): Sorry sonny—Can't take solids.
    The woman chuckles. MICK walks on, looking round. He sees the dishevelled girl with the man in her arms.
MICK (bending down): Hot soup?
    He looks at her: he recognises the face with horror.
MICK: My God! Patricia!
PATRICIA (smiling): Michael!

MICK: I thought you were going to marry the Duke of Belminster.
PATRICIA (gently stroking the man's face): This is the Duke of Belminster.
DICKIE BELMINSTER, raddled and bloated, sleeps in PATRICIA's lap. There is a sudden scream. A meths drinker has fallen into the fire. His body starts to burn. Women shriek. MICK drops everything and runs to pull him out of the fire. He is trying to beat out the flames when a hysterical woman runs up and beats him.
METHS DRINKER: You bugger! Leave him alone. Piss off! Piss off! He's my man! Leave him alone!
A big tramp comes up and grabs MICK by the shoulder.
BIG TRAMP: We don't want your filthy charity. Get back to school! Get out of here!
He throws MICK towards some of the other tramps standing near the fire.
TRAMPS: Piss off! Leave us alone!
MICK collects himself, looks about him, starts to call out wildly:
MICK: Listen friends...
WOMAN: Go back to Nanny!
MICK: Comrades!
TRAMP: Join the army!
MICK: Listen to me! Brothers!
The tramps shout mockingly at MICK—'Brothers!' MICK runs to some other tramps sitting near the fire.
MICK: You're men. You must realise it... (He moves along the small line of tramps): Men... Mankind. Brothers!... it's the only truth!
The old drunk tramp with the laughing woman stands waving his bottle.
OLD TRAMP: Truth.... This is the only truth... you bastard!
MICK comes closer to him. He speaks desperately.
MICK: No—it's you—me —all of us. We're all there is. Only man exists.
With shrieks of mocking laughter, three women dash forward and grab MICK's carrier-bag. They make off with it, scattering MICK's things and laughing insanely to themselves.
MICK: Man! Listen to it! What a marvellous word. Isn't it a marvellous word? It's fantastic! We must respect it. We must respect each other.

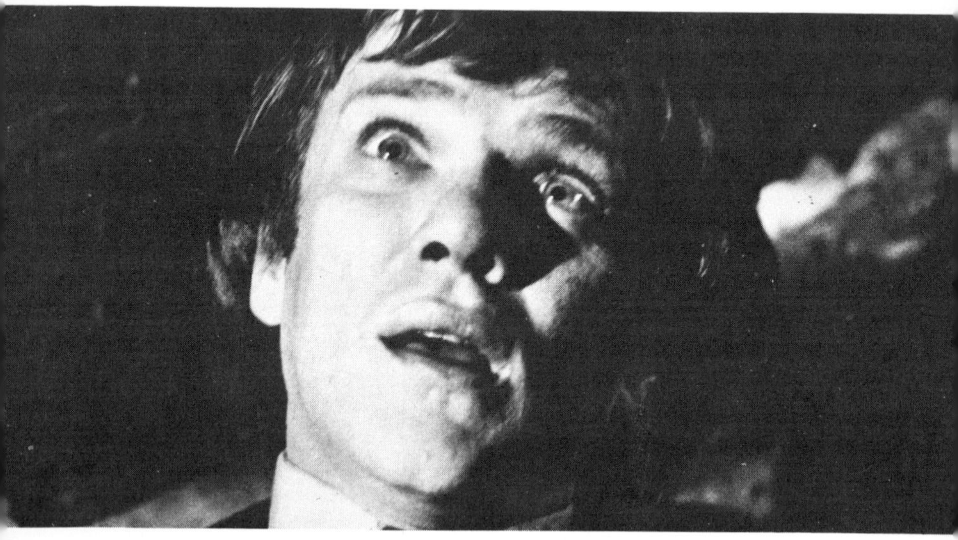

MICK is completely carried away now, a *possessed* evangelist. Slowly the tramps surround him. They start to pull his clothes off.

MICK : Not charity. Not pity. But dignity. Respect. I know. I swear it.

MICK struggles to keep on his feet. They remove his overcoat.

MICK (disappearing) : We must love one another. Love!

The tramps are tearing at MICK now. He breaks free. He runs through the fires, pursued by the shouting, waving tramps. Some of the other derelicts now get to their feet and join in the chase.

MICK runs along beside the low brick wall into the darkness of the bomb site. The derelicts shout mockingly as they pursue him. When they catch up with him they start pelting him with anything they can lay their hands on. MICK attempts to shield himself.

MICK (shouting) : Brothers!

The derelicts continue to hurl mud and stones at him. He tries to shield his face with his hands.

MICK (still shouting) : Brothers! Brothers! Brothers!

MICK is forced back. Suddenly he misses his footing and finds himself precipitated into a large pit. He ends up on his back, blinking up at the sky. All the derelicts crowd along the edge of the pit. They stare menacingly down at him. MICK stares back piteously. A noise makes him turn his head. Three of the derelicts have got hold of a huge oil drum. They send it rolling down the slope from the edge of the pit. Thundering, it careers down towards MICK, and into the camera.

BLACKOUT

REHEARSAL ROOM

ALAN, now wearing his fur coat and cap, sings *Changes*.

ALAN (singing) : *Everyone is going through changes,*
No one knows what's going on,
Everybody changes places,
But the world still carries on.

Love must always turn to sorrow
And everyone must play the game.
It's here today and gone tomorrow
But the world goes on the same.

■□ Everybody changes places
■ Tout le monde change de place
■ 大家挪在遷移
■ Люди двигаются с места на место
■ Von Platz zu Platz ein jeder treibt
■ みなが持場シ変えあラ
■ Tutti cambiano posto
■ كل فرد يتبادل المراكز غيره

During the song, the camera moves back to include the other members of the group. They are dressed as if for moving on...

TITLES
The words of the first verse appear, line by line, in nine different languages.

ALLEY OFF LEICESTER SQUARE
The camera moves down the side of a dark building to an alley where MICK, exhausted and unkempt, is walking alone past dustbins and rubbish. The song continues.

ALAN (voice over): *Now love must always turn to sorrow*
And everyone must play the game.
It's here today and gone tomorrow,
But the world goes on the same...

As the music comes to an end, MICK stands for a moment looking at the brassy glitter of London's West End. People mill about beneath the lights. A steady flow of traffic.

LEICESTER SQUARE
MICK walks into the square and stands in front of a window displaying a pop music album with its front cover of an androgynous singer. Passers-by move past busily. He stands looking round and up at the lights. An electronic newscaster announces: 'UNITED STATES: THREE YOUNG MEN HAVE BEEN FOUND SHOT DEAD ON A NEW YORK . . .' As MICK stares up at the moving sign, he is bumped into the stream of passers-by.

SHAFTESBURY AVENUE
MICK shuffles along the busy street. Youngsters mill about on corners. MICK passes a restaurant and a bar, then he turns and sees the moving newscaster again: 'SOVIET AIRLINER CRASHES AT ROME AIRPORT—NO SURVIVORS.' MICK wanders on past a café. He pauses and digs into a litter bin. The newscaster flashes on: 'TROOPS AND TERRORISTS CLASH IN BENGAL FAMINE AREA . . .' MICK walks on past the discotheques, theatres, cafés and cinemas. He stoops to pick up a cigarette butt, which he puts in his top pocket. He stops a smartly-dressed man, perhaps to ask him for

money. The man, embarrassed, detaches himself and quickly moves on.

MICK rests for a moment against a car: people heedlessly stream past. Down the pavement, under a canopy of lights, the top half of a sandwich board sways above the sea of heads. Scarlet letters announce: 'WANT TO BE A STAR?' A YOUNG MAN, scruffy and unshaved, is handing out leaflets. The lower half of the board has another message: 'STAR WANTED—TRY YOUR LUCK!' MICK moves towards the YOUNG MAN and takes a leaflet from him. The YOUNG MAN looks at him directly.

YOUNG MAN: Try your luck!

As the YOUNG MAN moves on, MICK looks back at him. Does he recognise his old gold suit? Is he reminded of the YOUNG MAN, first cocky, then dying behind the wheel of his scarlet sports car? Or of the YOUNG MAN grafted onto a pig's body in PROFESSOR MILLAR's clinic? This YOUNG MAN turns, as if conscious of MICK's stare, and looks back at him with a strange intensity....

AUDITION HALL

A white screen. Young men (heads-and-shoulders) appear in front of it and are photographed by flashlight. The hall is large and high. Benches, crowded with young men of every description, are ranged across the floor with a central aisle. At the far end tables are set up on a stage. At these are seated five or six men and women, consulting notes or scripts and surveying the benches. Prominent is the DIRECTOR, in scarlet jersey-shirt and black leather coat (we have seen him before, in the first musical number at the beginning of the film); he confers with the CASTING DIRECTOR beside him, a sensitive lady in dark glasses. Just in front of the doorway a girl (PATRICIA?) is sitting at a trestle table, listing the arrivals and handing each a questionnaire. MICK arrives in front of her.

GIRL: Name.
MICK: Michael Travis...
GIRL: Availability?
MICK: Available.

She writes down his particulars. He takes his form and walks on to join the others sitting on the benches. After a few paces, he looks back at the GIRL. She turns, feeling his stare, and looks at him. She gives nothing away. MICK walks on down the aisle. A young man rises out of the crowded benches to go forward to be interviewed. MICK goes to take his place, then pauses a moment glancing at him. He reminds him of MACINTYRE. MICK sits down. He looks at the young man seated next to him. He too reminds him of somebody. . . . He looks round at the man behind him. . . . He seems to remember him as well. . . Up on the stage, the DIRECTOR's eyes are straying through the ranks of the young men. He lifts up his glasses and leans towards the CASTING DIRECTOR beside him. He speaks. She looks at MICK and nods. He leans across to his ASSISTANT on the other side and speaks to him. Their eyes are on MICK.

The ASSISTANT comes down to where MICK is seated and taps him on the shoulder. MICK rises, puzzled. He looks at the ASSISTANT strangely. Some sense of recognition is stirring. He is escorted up the aisle to the white screen.

ASSISTANT: Now what we'd like you to do is stand in front of this screen . . . and I'll let you know what to do in a minute.

MICK stands in front of the screen. He blinks in the sudden glare of flashlights.

THE DIRECTOR stands, picks up his script and runs down the steps from the stage, followed by the CASTING DIRECTOR. The DIRECTOR stands in front of MICK.

A clapper board comes across MICK's face. It reads:

O LUCKY MAN!

DIR:—	CAM:—
LINDSAY ANDERSON	MIROSLAV ONDRICEK
SCENE 755	TAKE 1
16/6/72	NIGHT INTERIOR

DIRECTOR (to his ASSISTANT): Books.

He inspects MICK, eyes half-closed, as the ASSISTANT presents MICK with an armful of books.

ASSISTANT: Now hold these under your right arm, will you.

MICK takes the books and stands erect. A camera flashes. The DIRECTOR nods his head.

DIRECTOR: Good. . . . Gun.

The books are taken from MICK and he is given a Bren gun. He poses with it, rather tentatively.

DIRECTOR: More aggressive. . .

MICK tries. More flashes. He winces, nervously.

DIRECTOR: Right.
> The Bren gun is taken away. The DIRECTOR takes a step forward from the group.

DIRECTOR: Now smile.
MICK: I beg your pardon?
DIRECTOR (authoritatively): Smile.
MICK: Why?
DIRECTOR: Just do it.
MICK: I'm afraid I can't smile without a reason.
DIRECTOR (insistent): Smile!
MICK (irritated now): What's there to smile about?
DIRECTOR: Just do it!
MICK: Why?
DIRECTOR (gravely): Don't ask why.
MICK (loudly): What's there to smile *about*...?
> The DIRECTOR pauses a little moment, then raises his arm suddenly. He strikes MICK firmly across the head with his script.

BLACKOUT

> The DIRECTOR looks gravely at MICK.

BLACKOUT

> MICK, dazed, lifts his head. His eyes find the camera. His face clears. His look is not thoughtful, but direct, comprehending. The camera moves in. A faint smile begins to break at the corner of his mouth... the smile of UNDERSTANDING? or of OBEDIENCE? The camera zooms into a close-up of MICK's face as we hear the beginning of the song, *O Lucky Man!*

ALAN: *If you have a friend on whom you think you can rely—*
> *You are a lucky man!*

BLACKOUT

> On stage, ALAN, now dressed in a black velvet suit and bow-tie, is singing at a piano.

ALAN: *And if you've found the reason to live on and not to die—*
> *You are a lucky man!*

> MICK, wearing his gold suit with bow-tie, turns and smiles radiantly.

ALAN: *The preachers and the poets and the scholars don't know it,*

The hall is full of people, standing watching, smiling, starting to dance. MICK is in the centre. The DIRECTOR approaches; he shakes MICK's hand warmly and they embrace. Then Mary Macleod (MRS BALL) comes up and embraces MICK, followed by Rachel Roberts (GLORIA ROWE) and then Helen Mirren (PATRICIA). Everyone is happy, breaking into dance. Other characters start to dance joyously to the music.

ALAN : *The temples and the statues and the steeples don't show it,*
  If you've got the secret just try not to blow it—
    Stay a lucky man! Stay a lucky man!

We cut back to ALAN at the piano.

ALAN : *Because on and on and on and on we go,*

MICK holds PATRICIA and they dance off into the crowd. They dance past MR DUFF with BECKY, and then on past PROFESSOR MILLAR with the PEASANT GIRL.

ALAN : *And it's around the world in circles turning,*
  Earning what we can
  While others dance away the chance to light your day—

The dancers have begun to circle around. We glimpse many of the characters from earlier sequences in the film. We cut back to ALAN singing :

ALAN : *So you know that if you have a friend on whom you think*
              you can rely,
  You are a lucky man!

First MICK dancing, exhilerated. Then PATRICIA. The JUDGE dances with the USHER; GLORIA ROWE with WILLIAM. ALAN PRICE sings...

ALAN : *And if you've found the reason to live on and not to die,*
  You are a lucky man!
  You know the preachers and the poets and the scholars
              don't know it...

The camera moves over the dancers. In the crowd, we glimpse JENKINS dancing with the TEA LADY, MR DUFF with BECKY, then MRS NAIDU with the CHAIRMAN. Then back to ALAN singing...

ALAN : *And the temples and the statues and the steeples won't*
                show it,
  If you've got the secret, just try not to blow it—
    Stay a lucky man! Stay a lucky man!

The camera whirls past the circling dancers, now moving one after the other in an endless chain.

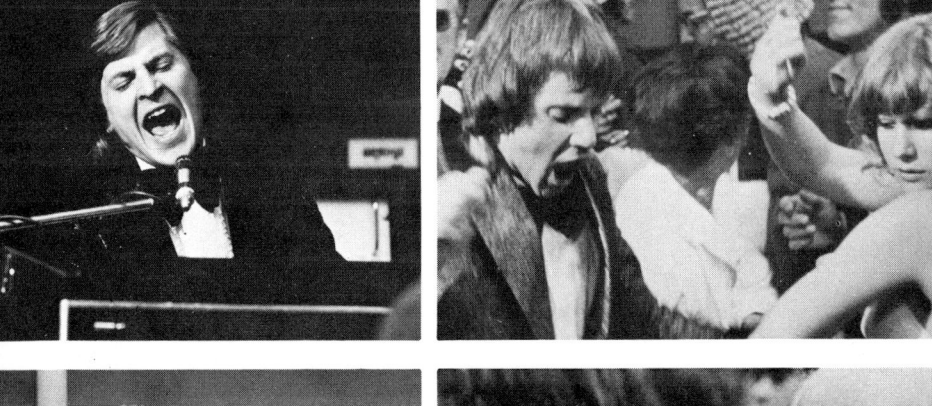

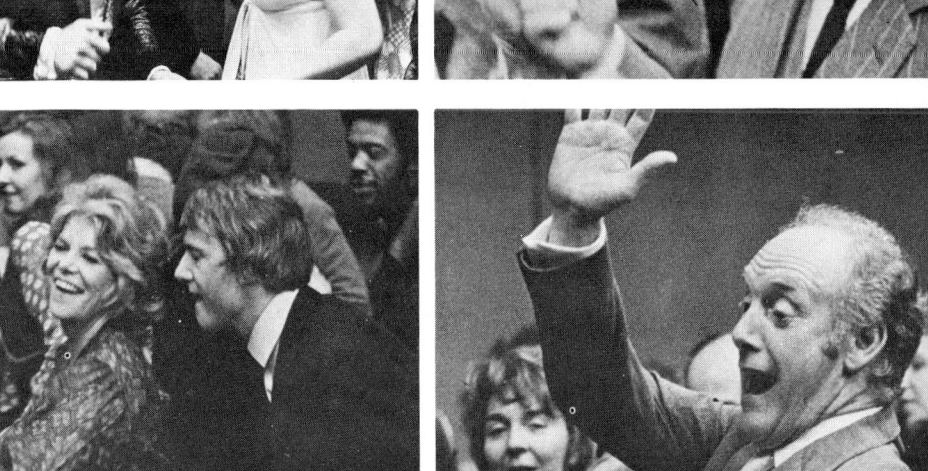

Alan : And it's around and round and round and round and
round we go,
And it's around the world in circles turning,
Earning what we can...
While others dance away the chance to light your day—
So it's on and on and on, and it's on and on and on
Around the world in circles turning...

Balloons drop from the ceiling onto the dancing crowd, who jump, snatch and grab, trying to catch them. Mick is in the centre.

Alan : ... Earning what we can
While others dance away the chance to light your day.

As the song and the film end, we iris in through the tumult of people and balloons, on to Mick, still dancing, still reaching out....